LYDIA KNIGHT'S HISTORY

By

SUSA YOUNG GATES

Lydia Knight's History
by Susa Young Gates

ISBN: 978-93-59320-58-8

Published by

DOUBLE 9 BOOKS

2/13-B, Ansari Road, Daryaganj
New Delhi – 110002
info@double9books.com
www.double9books.com
Tel. 011-40042856

ABOUT THE AUTHOR

Susa Gates (March 18, 1856 – May 27, 1933) was an American writer, periodical editor, president of the Daughters of Utah Pioneers, and campaigner for women's rights. She was the daughter of Brigham Young, the head of the LDS Church. Gates published numerous short stories, novels, poetry, and other literary works throughout her life. Gates wrote more than other Mormon writers, according to R. Paul Cracroft's argument. Gates was also active in the Church of Jesus Christ of Latter-day Saints (LDS Church), where she created lesson manuals, served on the Relief Society general board, led genealogy work, and served as a missionary, among other things. Brigham Young's twenty-second wife, Lucy Bigelow, gave birth to Gates at Salt Lake City, Utah Territory. Gates was born Susanna but went by Susa for the majority of her life. She was Brigham's forty-second child and Lucy Bigelow and Brigham Young's second child. Gates was raised in the Lion House. Because of the size of her father's family, Young's home life was quite regulated. Her days were structured around planned meals, prayers, schooling, family devotionals, and sleep. According to Gates, she had a pleasant upbringing and enjoyed growing up in the Young family.

CONTENTS

PREFACE

The growing demand for our own literature among the youth of this people has induced us to undertake the publication of a new series of books. The general satisfaction which the books of the Faith-Promoting Series have given, encourages us in the hope that this new series, which is designed to contain various items of interest and instruction from the lives of our noble sisters, will also be worthy of the perusal of the Saints.

We present, as the first book of the Noble Women's Lives Series, the history of a lady who early joined the Church, and remained faithful through the various trials and hardships to which the early Saints were subjected. And now, when in the evening of life, her influence is still being felt for good in Zion. The history of such persons should be written that the young may be stimulated to emulate their noble examples.

That this little work may prove both entertaining and instructive to those into whose hands it may come is the earnest desire of

The Publisher.

CHAPTER I

A little girl with light-blue eyes and fair hair sat under the shade of the forest trees pulling a sheep-skin. One by one her brothers and sisters, older and younger than she, had grown weary of the work and wandered off to play.

"Oh, Lydia, how can you sit there over that tiresome work. Look at the shadows under the trees, and the squirrels calling to us to come and chase them from limb to limb. Let's have a play," said the last little boy as his patience at length had ebbed away.

"No," replied the fair-haired maiden, and the firm little mouth took another line of determination as she spoke, "I shall not leave the sheepskin till the last lock is pulled."

A "clearing" in the forest of the western part of New York State, a large comfortable cabin on a rise of ground near the center of the space, with wide-open doors and floors of gleaming white, waving grain on one side of the house and a large vegetable garden on the other side constituted the scene of a home in the forest wilds, which was a common one in those days—the years between 1810 and 1820. The circle of high waving trees gave a grandeur and beauty to the view that nothing else could possibly do.

The little girl who sat so steadily at work had been brought by her parents two years previously to this wild western home.

She was born in 1812, in Sutton, Worcester Co., Mass., and eight happy years had been spent in her earliest home.

Shall I tell you about her father, whose name was Jesse Goldthwait? He was a medium-sized, well-built New Englander, prudent, industrious and the possessor of a firm will. Her mother was a quiet-spoken woman, but she bad an ardent temperament and a great deal of natural refinement. She had had some scholastic advantages and was exceedingly ambitious for her children. Five sisters and six brothers had Lydia, and a very happy and peaceful family they were.

Don't you know what "wool-pulling" is? Well, while my little girl is finishing her work I will tell you:

When the sheep was killed for family use, the skin was rolled up by the thrifty farmers in ashes or lime and laid away for some time. Then the wool could easily be separated from the hide. This last piece of labor generally fell to the children. And in Jesse Goldthwait's family none of the children would keep to the work but Lydia. So that it soon passed into a proverb, when Lydia exhibited that determination in anything which was so striking a point in her character, they would say to each other:

"It's no use trying to make her give up her design. You know Lydia never leaves till the last lock is pulled."

The years passed on and Lydia grew apace. But as she attained to early womanhood, she did not lose the slender form, the quiet voice she had inherited from her mother, or the firm will her father had bequeathed to her. She was brought up to habits of work and she had also received religious training from her parents.

When the girl was about fifteen years old, a council was held concerning her by her father and mother:

"Let us send the girl to school, father: you are comfortable for means, and Lydia is a good, obedient girl."

"That she is," replied the father, "and studiously inclined. I will think it over, mother."

After some deliberation, a boarding-school was chosen, and the girl placed under proper care.

Who cannot fancy the life of a school-girl of fifteen? Happy, careless as to the future, mindful of the husking-bees and quiltings, and with bright, shy glances for the youths who begin to "wish to see you home."

Among Lydia's acquaintances in the village where she was attending school, was a young man whose name was Calvin Bailey. One who was a stranger in the village, but his smart, dapper ways, and his smooth address won him many friends among the thoughtless, the youth and the pleasure-loving of the villagers.

"He is *so* nice," said the girls.

"Calvin is the right sort of a fellow for a frolic," added the young men.

Lydia admired the young man in common with the rest of her companions, and was far too young, too much of a child to dread the very smoothness which so often covers a wicked heart.

The Winter passed into Spring and Lydia returned to her home.

That Summer in her happy home was one long to be remembered by the girl who was fast hastening to so different an experience in life.

The rides with her brothers, the hunts in the forest for nuts, for cones, for flowers and for rare ferns, the quiet, happy talks with her mother, the lovely Sabbath evenings when Father Jesse would solemnly tell of the mysteries of God. All these home joys were hardly appreciated at the time, but long after remembered with sharp pangs of agony.

When the Winter came, she returned to her school, and now the acquaintance already began with young Bailey, ripened into a mutual attachment, and in the Fall of 1828 the couple were married.

For a little time all went well. But the old, old story was told again. The story of a man's cruelty and a woman's suffering.

The young man was one who "drank occasionally." Had he been accused of being a drunkard he would have been highly insulted! But the misery of the poor girl was just as real as though things received their right names and "a spade be called a spade." Shall I attempt to picture her sufferings? The long, lonely hours of waiting, the longing dread to hear the stumbling footsteps, the tortures of fear, the vile abuse, the bitter cursings heaped upon her head, the vain regrets, the puny hopes of a better life born but to be strangled by the next night's waiting agony, the gradual benumbing, crushed feeling that life was made but for suffering—shall I tell of this? No! for those who are waiting and watching for the unsteady step know all I can tell, and they who have never borne the dreadful burden would not understand me.

This firm, quiet wife endured it all in silence. The home they owned was some distance from her father's, and she was too sensitive to complain of one whom she called by the sacred name of husband.

In 1829, a little girl was born, and this great blessing soothed the aching heart of the youthful mother.

The months and years went on, and one morning when Lydia had been married about three years, she woke up to find herself alone, deserted by her husband, poor and almost friendless. What should she do? What could she do? The only course open to her was to return to her father's home; but this was a little trial to her proud spirit. Still it was all that was left for her to do; and taking her little girl by the hand, she entered her parents' home and begged their sympathy and support. She did not ask in vain; the farmer and his wife wept at her sorrow, but gladly took her to their arms once more.

In six months after her return, a little boy was born to her, Feb. 1832, but died almost at its birth.

The girl was quieter, sadder and more subdued than ever. Her work was well done but no light laughter went with it. Tears were often in her eyes, and a constant aching was at her heart.

One year passed away, and in January, 1833, the little girl, her mother's only comfort, was taken ill and died. The mother felt she had indeed drank the last bitter drop from sorrow's cup. She little dreamed of the grand drama of the future, in which she was to act so noble a part. God alone could soothe or heal the wound, and He did.

CHAPTER II

Snow on the fields, on the hills and in the valleys. Snow on the house-tops and in the crevices. White, soft, dazzling snow.

The scene without was lovely beyond description. The trees weighted down with their crown of glory. But within, the inmates of the farm were comparatively prisoners.

"My dear," the mother said to her husband, "Lydia is full of sorrow. Her thoughts are far from her works; I fear for her unless something can be done to draw her mind from her trouble."

"Well, wife, these things are beyond our power Lydia will be all right in time."

"Pray God it may be so," she fervently replied.

In February, 1833, a young man who had been reared near Lydia's birthplace, by the name of Nikerson, paid a visit to the Goldthwaits.

In reply to their friendly questions, he told them he had settled in Upper Canada, had married the finest little woman in the kingdom, and was getting wealthy at merchandizing.

"What ails Lydia?" he asked one day.

"She is ill and full of sorrow." And then the sad story was told. And at its close, the young man sat silent for some time with tears of sympathy in his eyes for the poor young creature.

Finally, looking up, he said: "I'll tell you what, Mrs. Goldthwait, let me take that girl home with me, and I'll warrant my wife and I will bring back the roses to her cheeks, if kindness and comfort can do it. Don't you think a change of scenery and travel, with all its distractions, will occupy her mind to the exclusion of other things?"

"I am sure the change of climate would be of benefit, if we could get father and Lydia to consent to it," replied the mother. So after much consultation, it was arranged that when Mr. Nickerson returned, Lydia should go with him.

They started out in the last of February, and traveled by sleigh. The usual route to Canada, was down to Buffalo, across the Niagra river, then on up the lake shore. Mr. Nickerson's home was situated about the middle on the Canada side of the lake some distance from the shore, and he thought that by crossing the lake on the ice, he would save a hundred miles travel. They stopped at a hotel about twenty five miles above Buffalo on the Lake Erie shore, and although told that no one had ventured to ride over that winter, he was determined to go across. So one bright sunny morning they started. Fifteen of the twenty miles were traversed in speed and safety, when lo! they were stopped by a fissure in the ice about two feet wide, and stretching up and down as far as the eye could see. The ice was, of course, thin on the edges. But out, and over the chasm jumped the venturesome young man, and after stamping around and trying the temper of the frozen floor, he decided it would be all plain sailing when once across. This determined, he made a spring for the side where Lydia sat in the sleigh. One, two, three, over he goes, — but oh, horrible! the ice gives way and down he goes into the dark, silent waters beneath. Instinctively he threw one arm out, and resting it on the shelf of ice above him, succeeded in gradually drawing himself up on the ice. Nothing could turn him from his purpose, however, and accordingly he unhitched the horse, made him jump across, pushed the sleigh, with the trembling girl seated in it, after the horse, jumped over once more himself, and was soon under way again. Save that his clothes were frozen on him, neither Mr. Nickerson nor his companion felt any bad effects from their adventure. Reaching a hotel, they soon warmed and rested. From there to Mount Pleasant, which was his home, no incident occurred worthy of note.

Arriving at the house, Mrs. Nickerson met the travelers with a hearty welcome, and in the kind, thoughtful attention of this worthy couple, the sore heart of the patient girl was soothed and rested. The complete change of the mode of living, scenery and people had its effect upon her, and she grew more resigned day by day to her broken life.

The people who lived in the thriving little village were hospitable and kind. They were mostly Methodists. A man by the name of McIntyre, who was a class leader, induced Lydia to take a Sunday school class, and she was much interested in her labors in this direction.

The Spring and Summer came and passed away and Fall came. Few strangers visited the little village and life passed quietly on.

One day in October, 1833, a wagon load of people stopped at the door, and great was the surprise of all, when the party proved to be old Mr., and Mrs. Nickerson and the youngest son, Levi, who, of course, was Freeman's brother. They had with them two strange men. But we will let another chapter tell who and what they were.

CHAPTER III

Although so remote from the States, rumors of a new prophet and a "golden bible" had reached Mount Pleasant, and had been wondered over and commented upon.

Freeman had been told that his parents had joined the new Church, and he was rather disgusted with the information.

It will be necessary to say here that the old gentleman was indeed full of the gospel he had embraced, and was so anxious for the eternal welfare of his sons in Canada, that he had hitched up his carriage, gone on a visit to Kirtland and prevailed upon the Prophet Joseph Smith and Elder Sidney Rigdon to accompany him on a visit to his sons, Moses and Freeman, in Mount Pleasant.

These two brethren were the strangers who were with the aged parents.

"Well father," said Freeman when told who they were, "I will welcome them for your sake, but I would just about as soon you had brought a nest of vipers and turned them loose upon us."

Moses and Freeman were wealthy merchants and men of influence in Mount Pleasant. On the evening of the arrival, after the bustle of welcome and a warm supper were over, everyone was too tired to talk, so all retired to rest. Next morning many were the curious glances that Lydia cast at this strange man who dared to call himself a prophet.

She saw a tall, well-built form, with the carriage of an Apollo, brown hair, handsome blue eyes, which seemed to dive down to the innermost thoughts with their sharp, penetrating gaze, a striking countenance, and with manners at once majestic yet gentle, dignified yet exceedingly pleasant.

Elder Rigdon was a middle-aged man of medium hight, stout and quite good-looking, but without the noble grandeur that was so distinguishing a mark of the prophet.

The day was spent by the travelers in examining a fine new store which had just been erected by the Nickerson brothers, and in looking around the premises as also in walking through the village itself.

The Elders were very wise. They said nothing about their views or doctrines, but waited patiently until some one should express an interest.

As evening drew near Mr. Nickerson became anxious to hear something of the newcomer's faith.

"Oh," said he, "just let him talk; I'll silence him if he undertakes to talk about the Bible. I guess I know as much about the scriptures as he does."

This was to his wife whom he directed to place the family Bible on the table in the parlor.

As soon as supper was over, he invited his visitors and family to go up stairs to the parlor, where he said they would have some talk. All, accordingly, repaired to the large well-furnished room, and then Mr. N. said to the Prophet:

"Now, Mr. Smith, I wish you and Mr. Rigdon to speak freely. Say what you wish and tell us what you believe. We will listen."

Turning to his wife, he whispered, "now you'll see how I shall shut him up."

The Prophet commenced by relating the scenes of his early life. He told how the angel visited him, of his finding the plates, the translation of them, and gave a short account of the matter contained in the Book of Mormon.

As the speaker continued his wonderful narrative, Lydia, who was listening and watching him intently, saw his face become white and a shining glow seemed to beam from every feature.

As his story progressed he would often allude to passages of scripture. Then Mr. N. would speak up and endeavor to confound him. But the attempt was soon acknowledged even by himself to be futile.

The Prophet bore a faithful testimony that the Priesthood was again restored to the earth, and that God and His Son had conferred upon him the keys of the Aaronic and Melchisedek Priesthoods. He stated that the last dispensation had come, and the words of Jesus were now in force—"Go ye into all the world and preach the gospel to every creature. He that believeth and is baptized shall be saved; but he that believeth not shall be damned."

Elder Rigdon spoke after the Prophet ceased. He related some of his early experiences, and told those present that he had received a testimony for himself of the truth of what Joseph had said, and then exhorted all present to take the advice of the ancient Apostle James, and ask God, and the testimony would be given to each one; for God is the same now as He was anciently, and has communicated His only gospel to men. "God," said Elder Rigdon, "is no respecter of persons, but will give to all that ask of Him a knowledge of the things Joseph Smith has declared unto you whether they are true or false, of God or of man."

You may be sure that by this time Mr. N. was quite willing to sit and listen, saying but little to interrupt or confound.

After both men were through speaking, many questions were asked by all present for information. The listeners were honest-hearted people, and when truth is told to such, they are constrained to accept and believe.

"And is this then," said Mr. N., "the curious religion the newspapers tell so much about? Why if what you have just said is not good sound sense, then I don't know what sense is."

A feeling of agreeable disappointment was felt by Mr. N. and family that these strange men were so different to the various representations of them.

Seldom have any petitions been sent up to heaven more fervent and earnest than were those of the inhabitants of Mr. N.'s home that night.

Next day notice was sent out that there would be public preaching in the Nickerson Bros', new store-house. A large and attentive audience was present.

Elder Sidney Rigdon spoke to the people with great clearness on the first principles of the gospel, and closed with a strong testimony to the truth of so-called "Mormonism."

The Prophet then arose and poured forth a golden stream of words, many of which were verily pearls without price. Setting forth the restoration of the gospel and the great work that had commenced on the earth. With power he exhorted every one who was present to seek for the truth of his and his companion's words from the source of all light, all truth, all religion, and a knowledge of the truth of the same should surely follow.

Great was the excitement among the peaceful dwellers in Mount Pleasant.

The next day Mr. N. and wife, his father and mother, accompanied by the two strangers, went a distance of ten miles to visit some particular friends and tell them of these wonderful things they had heard and by this time fully believed.

Returning the following day, religious services were again held in the Nikerson store-house.

A large and attentive audience listened to all that was said, and at the close of the meeting several persons came forward and requested baptism.

The day following a meeting was again held, and after it was over the Prophet baptized twelve persons, among whom was Lydia Bailey, Mr. N.

and all of his household. She who was always so sober and full of reflection had received the glad message with trembling joy. She was filled with a bright, peaceful influence and was full of gratitude that God had spared her to hear and accept His glorious gospel. How often we wish and even pray for that which would be our greatest misfortune! The lonely girl had thought of death and its rest with a longing heart, but now, why here was life, life eternal! Life filled to the utmost with good works, joy, and happiness. No matter what should come now, she should know it was all for the best. That is one of the greatest charms of our holy religion. Whatever is, is always for the best if we are only true and pure.

So into the water goes Lydia with a light step and happy heart. She was so filled with the Holy Ghost while standing in the water after she was baptized that she was constrained to cry aloud,

"Glory to God in the highest! Thanks be to His holy name that I have lived to see this day and be a partaker of this great blessing."

In the evening, the new members of the Church assembled in Mr. N.'s house for confirmation. God bestowed His Spirit very freely and the Prophet gave much valuable instruction.

Two more persons came to the Prophet and requested baptism at the meeting the next day. It was attended to and a branch of the Church was organized. Freeman Nickerson was ordained as the presiding Elder.

The evening of this day (which was the seventh day, the Prophet had been there, and came on Monday, October 24, 1833), the family were all seated around the wide, old-fashioned fire-place in the parlor listening to the Prophet's words and full of rejoicing.

"I would be so glad if some one who has been baptized could receive the gift of tongues as the ancient Saints did and speak to us," said Moses Nickerson.

"If one of you will rise up and open your mouth it shall be filled, and you shall speak in tongues," replied the Prophet.

Every one then turned as by a common instinct to Lydia, and said with one voice, "Sister Lydia rise up."

And then the great glory of God was manifested to this weak but trusting girl. She was enveloped as with a flame, and, unable longer to retain her seat, she arose and her mouth was filled with the praises of God and His glory. The spirit of tongues was upon her, and she was clothed in a shining light, so bright that all present saw it with great distinctness above the light of the fire and the candles.

The visitors had desired to return on the next day, which was Tuesday. Accordingly, preparations were made for their departure. It was decided that the Prophet and Elder Rigdon should return by crossing Lake Erie, Freeman giving them the money to do so. They all started out together— old Mr. and Mrs. Nickerson, and Joseph and Sydney. The journey was thus shortened by two or three hundred miles for the Prophet and his companion.

That morning, while the team was being hitched up, Joseph paced back and forth in the sitting room in deep study. Finally he spoke up and said:

"I have been pondering on Sister Lydia's lonely condition, and wondering why it is that she has passed through so much sorrow and affliction and is thus separated from all her relatives. I now understand it. The Lord has suffered it even as He allowed Joseph of old to be afflicted, who was sold by his brethren as a slave into a far country, and through that became a savior to his father's house and country. Even so shall it be with her, the hand of the Lord will overrule it for good to her and her father's family."

Turning to the young girl he continued: "Sister Lydia, great are your blessings. The Lord, your Savior, loves you, and will overrule all your past sorrows and afflictions for good unto you. Let your heart be comforted. You are of the blood of Israel descended through the loins of Ephraim. You shall yet be a savior to your father's house. Therefore be comforted, and let your heart rejoice, for the Lord has a great work for you to do. Be faithful and endure unto the end and all will be well."

Immediately after that the party set out, and left behind many warm and faithful friends.

The good work thus commenced continued with unabated vigor and numbers came forward and were baptized.

CHAPTER IV

Lydia remained here until the Summer of '34, and then, on seeing a chance to return within about eighty miles of her home in western New York, she did so. At a town called St. Catherine she remained some two months, and then went by stage to her father's house.

So beautiful was this gospel in the eyes of the ardent girl, that she felt that all that was needful for her parents to share in her joy, was simply to tell them the story. But as is often the case, the father and mother, although so good and kind, could not comprehend the truth.

"Lydia," said the mother, "you don't mean to tell me you have united yourself with those disgraceful Mormons. To think that my daughter should dishonor herself by being cheated and deluded by those imposters!"

"Oh, mother," the tearful Lydia replied, "don't call those great and good men imposters, whom I have had the honor to see and know. Indeed they are true gentlemen and earnest Christians. If you would only let me tell you of these great truths that have been revealed from heaven."

But arguments and tears were of no avail. Nothing could induce the indignant mother who was a strict Presbyterian, or the quiet father, who, although professing no religion, was conscientious and moral, to accept her views for one moment. On the other hand, the principles Lydia had embraced were too precious to be given up for father or mother, tenderly loved as they were.

"It's no use," at last said the mother, "you know Lydia never would leave the sheep-skin till the last lock was pulled."

The girl grew restless and unhappy under the constant railery and derision showered upon the despised religion by her parents, while, at the same time they gave much pity and sympathy to their poor deluded daughter.

At last she decided upon going out to Kirtland which was then the gathering place of the Saints. Seeing her so determined Mr. and Mrs. Goldthwait gave Lydia ample means to go to her destination, and be comfortable and respectable. In the Spring of '35, once more this lone woman started out on a journey.

On reaching Kirtland, the family with whom Lydia had traveled, set at once to make arrangements to settle down. Leaving his wife and Lydia at the hotel, Mr. Knight, for that was the gentleman's name, went out, soon returning with his brother Vincent, who was a resident of Kirtland. On being introduced to Lydia, Vincent Knight said: "Sister, the Prophet is in bondage and has been brought into distress by the persecutions of the wicked, and if you have any means to give, it will be a benefit to him." "Oh yes, sir," she replied, "here is all I have. I only wish it was more," emptying her purse, containing, perhaps fifty dollars, in his hand as she spoke.

He looked at it and counted it and fervently exclaimed: "Thank God, this will release and set the Prophet free!"

The young girl was without means now, even to procure a meal or a night's lodging. Still the sweet spirit that rested upon her whispered "all will be well."

As evening drew on, Vincent Knight returned and brought the welcome news that Joseph was at liberty, and Lydia's joy to think that she had been the humble means of helping the Prophet was unbounded.

After talking some time Vincent remarked to her: "Now sister, if you think you can be comfortable and happy with my family, you are welcome to a home there. You shall be as a sister to my wife and myself."

Was not here the promise of the spirit beautifully verified?

For six or eight months Lydia lived a pleasant life beneath this good man's roof.

In the Fall of '35, the Prophet's brother Hyrum requested Lydia to come to his home and assist his wife. He promised her she should receive all the care and thought that could be given to her if she really were at home. She complied with the request, and while living there became acquainted with one of the brethren who boarded at the place while working on the Kirtland Temple. His name was Newel Knight, although not related in any way with the Knight family spoken of in the beginning of this chapter. The young man was tall, had light brown, hair, a keen blue eye and a very energetic and determined manner.

"Brother Knight is a widower," remarked Sister Smith one day when she and Lydia were busily at work.

"Oh indeed," laconically replied the girl.

"Yes, poor fellow. He lost his wife last Fall. She was a delicate woman, and the many trials and persecutions she suffered were too much for her frail body, and she died when her baby was but two days old. The little one lived but a few hours. Poor Brother Knight! His heart was almost broken. He has a little boy three years old living with his aunt, Newel's sister. Poor fellow, he is very lonely."

Lydia went on with her work making no reply, although her heart ached with sympathy for the desolate young man; for was *she* not well acquainted with sorrow? did not she know the anguish of being alone?

But well she knew that friendly interest was all she could give to this noble man who had so plainly shown his interest in her.

One day as they sat alone together in the family room. Newel said to her kindly, very gently:

"My child, you seem very lonely as well as myself. Why can we not comfort each other?"

"Sir," she replied indignantly, "I know my condition is lonely and not a desirable one, but I do not wish you to insult me. I have not the slightest knowledge where my husband is, or whether he is alive or dead. But I do not wish to take any step to make my condition worse or bring shame upon my family and deprive me of the salvation I am seeking to obtain."

With these words she immediately left the room giving him no opportunity to make a reply.

Several days passed without giving Newel the chance he wished for to apologize and explain to the offended girl.

Meeting her at last he told her he was sorry to have incurred her displeasure, and endeavored to show her that according to the law she was a free woman, having been deserted for three years with nothing provided for her support. But all that he said had no influence on Lydia who replied calmly that she was of the same mind she had been a week previous. But love is not killed so easily. Newel continued to make every endeavor to persuade Lydia to relinquish her own feelings, and accept the freedom that the law offered; but Lydia remained firm.

The young man was finally so convinced that she could not be persuaded, and so full was he of the desire to have the woman he felt God had designed to be his wife, that he fasted and prayed three days and nights, and then sought the Prophet and presented the case to him, that he might get the word of the Lord. Accordingly, Joseph presented his petition to the Lord, and the reply came that Lydia was free from that man. God did not wish any good woman to live a life of loneliness, and she was free to marry. Also that the union of Newel and Lydia would be pleasing in His sight.

Full of joy Newel sought Lydia and communicated the word he had received. No longer need the lovely girl fight this love that had grown up in both hearts. Throwing herself on her knees she poured out her soul in thanksgiving to God for His precious blessings. How unworthy she felt! What a thrill of joy went through her when she was told God had spoken to His servant Joseph concerning her, His humble handmaiden. Thereafter she gave her consent to marry Newel, and in a few days the news came to her of her husband's death. Was not this a convincing testimony of the truth of Joseph's word?

CHAPTER V

It was the advice of both Brother Hyrum and his wife, Jerusha, that the marriage should take place at once, and, as Lydia's objections were all overruled, preparations were made immediately.

On the 23rd of November, 1835, was the day chosen. Brother and Sister Smith decided to have a wedding-supper and invite some guests. Accordingly, in the afternoon of the 22nd he set out to invite the friends of the family.

Going to father Smith's, he asked them all to be present. Hastening on to Joseph's house he acquainted him with what was to take place the following day, and then requested him to be present. As Hyrum was hurrying away, Joseph called out:

"Stop, Brother Hyrum, don't be in such a hurry. Where are you going now?"

"Oh, I can't stay, I must make haste, as I have to go down and ask Seymour Brunson to come up and marry them."

"Stop, Hyrum! I tell you to wait a moment. You need not go down and ask Brother Brunson, for I mean to marry that couple myself."

Hyrum looked at his brother in astonishment at this announcement, for heretofore those who wished to be married were obliged to employ either a justice of the peace or a licensed minister. The law of Ohio did not recognize the "Mormon" Elders as ministers, and it was a punishable offense for a lay man to officiate in that capacity. In fact, several Elders had been arrested and fined for the performance of this act. Seymour Brunson had been down in the southern part of the State where prejudice did not run so high and had obtained a license to perform the ceremony. Consequently the Saints employed him whenever there was a couple to be married.

"Very well," replied Hyrum, "you know best. We will be very glad to have you do so."

The evening of the 23rd, about a dozen people gathered in Brother Hyrum's parlor, all of them intimate friends of the Patriarch and his family.

The young couple stood up, and the Prophet arose and commenced the ceremony. At its close he pronounced them husband and wife by the authority of the Priesthood which he held.

Thus was the first marriage ceremony ever performed by the Prophet Joseph Smith. Here was laid the foundation stone of the grand structure of our marriage ceremony. The revelation of sealing was not given, but after he had united the two he blessed them with fervor. Then turning to the company he exclaimed:

"Our Elders have been wronged and prosecuted for marrying without a license. The Lord God of Israel has given me authority to unite the people in the holy bonds of matrimony. And from this time forth I shall use that privilege and marry whomsoever I see fit. And the enemies of the Church shall never have power to use the law against me."

And so it was. The following Sunday he married four couple in public meeting, and continued to do so until his martyrdom without being molested.

After Joseph had thus spoken, some of the company asked some questions and he continued to speak and instruct them on the principle of marriage. Much that was entirely new to the Saints was revealed in his conversation, and again Lydia saw that strange, brilliant light shine through his features, like the mellow radience of an astral lamp, only purer and brighter.

The guests parted that evening with many good wishes for the two, who had suffered so much and were now about to commence the ascent of life's steep hill together. But few misgivings were felt, however, as all knew how genuinely good both were.

The Patriarch gave Brother and Sister Knight a hearty invitation to remain with his family during the Winter, and not attempt to set up housekeeping until they removed to their western home. They gladly accepted his offer, and spent several busy, happy months in this pleasant home.

Newel continued his labors on the temple, and in the evenings attended the schools for the Elders, organized that they might receive instructions preparatory to their endowments. Occasionally a lecture would be given, and at it always would be found Brother and Sister Knight.

How glorious it was to live during those brief Winter months receiving light upon light, revelation upon revelation as it flowed from the prophetic lips of Joseph!

When the lower room of the temple was completed an invitation was issued to all the Saints to assemble on the 27th of March, 1836, to witness the dedication of the first temple that had been built to the name of the Lord in these days. On the appointed day a large congregation was gathered inside and outside the building.

At nine o'clock, services were commenced by Sidney Rigdon reading the ninty-sixth and twenty-fourth Psalms. Singing and prayer were then offered, after which a discourse was delivered by Elder Rigdon.

An intermission of twenty minutes was made between the morning and afternoon services; the people, however did not leave their seats. In the afternoon, after the usual preliminary exercises, Joseph made a short address, and called upon the various quorums to sustain the presidency of the Church and all those who were called to preside. After singing, Joseph offered the dedicatory prayer, which will be found in the Doctrine and Covenants, Sec. 109 of the new edition.

At the close of this sublime prayer the congregation shouted as with one voice, "Hosanna! hosanna! hosanna to God and the Lamb! amen! amen and amen!" The sacrament was then administered. F. G. Williams arose and testified that while the prayer was being offered, a personage came in and sat down between Father Smith and himself, and remained there during the prayer. He described his clothing and appearance.

Joseph said that the personage was Jesus, as the dress described was that of our Savior, it being in some respects different to the clothing of the angels.

David Whitmer testified to seeing angels present.

The services were closed by singing and prayer. The Saints enjoyed a glorious day, and the temple was filled, as Lydia says, with the glory of God.

Cannot we, who are of the later generation, picture to ourselves this grand meeting, when Jesus and His angels were present and the glory of God was felt like a burning fire? What privileges our fathers and mothers enjoyed! How blest were they! And as we look back, it seems to us that we could gladly partake of their many and severe trials if we might enjoy their glorious blessings.

After the dedication, partial endowments were given to the Elders, Newel receiving his with the rest of his quorum.

Shortly after this Brother Knight was released from his labors on the temple, and decided to return to his home in Clay Co., Mo.

But how were they to get home? Newel had received no remuneration for his year's labor on the temple, but he freely donated it to the cause of God.

One day as they were talking over this difficulty Lydia remarked, "If we only had the sum I gave to the Prophet when I first came in, we could fit ourselves out very comfortably."

"Why, did you give the Prophet some money? Well I'm sure I thank God that you were able to help him in his distress, and I have no fear but what God will remember us as you remembered His servant."

This faith was not in vain. The following day Joseph stepped in, and, after shaking hands, said,

"So, Newel, you are about to depart for your western home. Are you amply provided for? Are you not in rather straightened circumstances? I know how you have worked for nothing for the past year, and I know also that you will get your reward."

"Yes, Brother Joseph, we are rather cramped just now for means," replied Newel.

"Just so. Sister Lydia, I have not forgotten how generously you helped me when I was in trouble."

"Oh, Brother Joseph, I have never felt for one moment that you were under the slightest obligation to me; I was only too glad to be the humble instrument of your release from our enemies."

"All right, Sister Lydia. However, I shall remember you."

He then left the house, but returned again in a little while and placed in the hands of this worthy couple about double the sum Lydia had given him, telling them to fit themselves out, and go comfortably provided for to their new home.

This little act well illustrates the just, and, at the same time, generous character of our noble martyr.

Brother Hyrum Smith kindly provided them with a team and teamster to take them to the Ohio river, from which place they could take a steamer to their home.

Thus prepared, the couple started out, and in due time arrived at their home, finding little Samuel (Brother Knight's boy) and the rest of his relatives well, and very much pleased to see him and his young bride. Their life here will be given in another chapter.

A description of the Patriarch Hyrum Smith will be interesting to my readers, I am sure. When Lydia went to his house he was between thirty-five and forty years of age, tall, well-framed, with a fine, handsome countenance, and blue eyes, and his face was full of intelligence and spirit. His manner was dignified, but he was amiable and vivacious, and withal exceedingly courteous and fascinating to all with whom he ever had intercourse. He was really a worthy brother of the Prophet, and together they were a worthy pair.

Father Smith was the general Patriarch of the Church. Not many of his blessings are now preserved, so thinking it will prove of interest to the young, who never had the privilege of seeing this venerable man, the blessing given to Lydia just before she left Kirtland for Clay Co., is here given:

A PATRIARCHAL BLESSING,

BY JOSEPH SMITH, SEN.

For Lydia Knight, who was born in Sutton, Worcester Co., Mass., June 9th, 1812.

"Sister Knight, in the name of Jesus Christ, I lay my hands upon thy head and ask my Heavenly Father to give me wisdom and power to pronounce such things as shall be according to the mind of the Holy Spirit. I also ask God to prepare thee to receive blessings, and pour them into thy soul even a fullness; and to give thee wisdom to abide all things that shall come upon thee; and bless thee in thy out-goings and in thy in-comings. I seal a father's blessing upon thee and thy posterity. For thou shalt be a mother of many children. And thou shalt teach them righteousness, and have power to keep them from the power of the destroyer; and thy heart shall not be pained because of the loss of thy children, for the Lord shall watch over them and keep them. And your children shall be raised up for glory and be ornaments in the Church.

"Thou hast been afflicted much in thy past days, and thy heart has been pained. Many tears have fallen from thine eyes and thou hast wept much. But thou shalt be comforted. The Lord loves thee and has given thee a kind and loving companion for thy comfort. And your souls shall be knit together, and nothing shall be able to dissolve them. Neither distress nor death shall separate you. You shall be preserved in life, and go safely and speedily to the land of Zion. Thou shalt have a good passage, and receive an inheritance in Jackson county. Thou shalt also see thy friends in Zion, thy brothers and sisters, and rejoice with them in the glory of God. Angels shall minister unto thee; thy heart shall be comforted. Thou shalt receive all thy heart's desire. Thy soul shall be enlarged, and thou shalt stand to see Israel gather from their dispersion, the ten tribes come from the land of the north country; the heavens rend, and the Son of Man come in all the glory of His Father. And thou shalt rise to meet Him and reign with Him a thousand years, and thy offspring with thee. Great are thy blessings. I confirm blessings on thee in common with thy husband. Blessings of the earth, and all things which thou needest for thy comfort. And thou shalt be a mother in Israel. Thou shalt relieve the wants of the oppressed and minister to the needy. All needed blessings are thine. I seal them upon thee, and I seal thee up unto eternal life, in the name of Jesus. Amen.

"(Sylvester Smith, Scribe)."

I will not endeavor to point out the many wonderful prophecies in this blessing which have already been fulfilled, but will let events as they are related speak for themselves.

CHAPTER VI

A branch called the Colesville Branch had gone up to Jackson Co., Missouri, from New York, and this branch was presided over by Brother Newel, who had been called to this position by revelation. It was driven from Jackson Co. in the Fall of '33, and had settled in Clay Co. This then was the future home of Lydia. Newel's father, two brothers and three sisters were here. His aged mother was buried in Jackson, being the first Saint buried in Missouri.

Arriving at their farm, some days were spent in visiting around among their friends before Brother Newel and wife settled down to their daily duties.

Newel's aged aunt, Esther Culver was taken into the family and tenderly cared for until her death, which occurred in the following Fall.

But a few weeks passed, however, in this pleasant manner before Lydia took the ague. This did not, however, affect her spirit, for she was too much filled with the power of the gospel to sorrow over the trials which were given her.

On the 1st of December, '36, a little girl was born to Lydia; and once more she took up the cares and exquisite joys of motherhood. The little one was called Sally after her grandmother. After the birth of her child Lydia's health improved much; but when the child was two months old, the mother had a severe inflammatory fever fastened on her, and for nine days she was insensible. Friends were ready and willing to assist; a physician was called in, but notwithstanding this she rapidly sank until nearly all had lost hope in her recovery. Her devoted husband felt that he could not lose her, and once more be left a desolate, miserable man; he gave himself up to fasting and prayer, that the disease might be rebuked, until God heard his cries and granted his fervent desires.

She awoke as it were from a long troubled sleep, and asked the watchers for her baby. It was brought, and from that moment she was rapidly healed.

Newel designed moving his family to Far West in the Spring, but shortly after Lydia's illness, he himself was prostrated with a lung fever.

This illness was expensive, and when he began to get around he found himself sadly in arrears. In consequence they were unable to move in the Spring.

The following year served to set them straight with their creditors, and in February, 1837, they purchased forty acres of land from the government, in Caldwell Co., close to Far West.

On the 29th of April, 1838, a boy was born, who was named James Philander by Father Morley when eight days old.

On the 4th of July, 1838, a large assembly of the Saints came together in Far West to celebrate the day and to lay the corner stone of a temple. The glorious stars and stripes were swung to the breeze and joy was everywhere among the Saints. But has there ever been an attempt to erect a temple without the bitterest fellings of our enemies being aroused?

The outside element began to be very jealous. Mobs assembled and threatenings were heard. Several days after the celebration, a storm, fierce and mighty as the storm which was soon to break over its inhabitants, swept oyer Far West. The heavens were blackened with rolling, hurrying masses of clouds. Down through the darkened air flashed the lightning's arrow! Peals of thunder shook the very earth! In the midst of this horrid uproar, a sudden, swift flash and down fell the liberty pole.

"Oh liberty," exclaimed the Prophet, "is it thus thy proud head shall be brought low? The wicked will seek to trample thee in the dust, and uproot thee from the earth!"

This prophecy was sadly fulfilled. But we will see in what manner.

Far West was a lovely little town, with rich fields, the houses and barns full and comfortable. Boasts were made by the rapacious, murdering robbers that as soon as the crops were well matured, the ghastly scenes of Jackson county should be repeated, and they would take possession of the smiling homes of the Saints.

To carry this out was not so easy as had been the Jackson county tragedy; for the authorities of Caldwell county were our own people. Some new pretext must be made to wrest the power from those who held the reins of government.

The same political hatred of the solid unity of the "Mormons" was felt by our enemies then that is felt for us now. Polygamy had not been revealed then, and so did not exist in their imaginations to cast a flimsy pretext over their fiendish purposes. It was Satan against Christ!

The mob spread out into adjoining counties to poison the Missourians against the people. At the August election in Daviess county, loud threats were made that the "Mormons" should not vote. Some of the Saints however were determined to maintain their rights and went to the polls to do so. They were roughly assaulted and a skirmish ensued. The "Mormons," however, succeeded in casting their votes, which so enraged the mob that they immediately began to organize into parties of hundreds, in some instances even thousands, to plunder our fields and drive off the stock; they attacked men on the high-road, and if they caught a "Mormon," or one they fancied to be a Saint they would murder him. One man by the name of Carey was thus assaulted and was not even allowed to see his family until just before he expired. An old gentleman by the name of Tannor was attacked and his skull beaten in.

About the middle of October word was brought to Far West that the mob was assembled by hundreds about ten miles from Far West, at a little settlement on Crooked river, and assistance was wanted. About sixty men, who were a legal organized militia, started out under David Patten, and, reaching Crooked river, they were obliged to defend themselves and people from the mob. The little party was defeated and overpowered, six of our brethren falling martyrs, among whom was David Patten, one of the first quorum of the Twelve Apostles. Not many days elapsed ere a hurried messenger brought the startling news that just outside the city a mighty multitude was camped with full intent to raze the town to the ground.

The next morning Joseph sent out a flag of truce to learn the intentions of this vast mob.

They were met by another flag of truce, and the two messengers conferred together.

"What is your purpose? What is the intention of those you represent? Why have you thus come to alarm and terrify the peaceful dwellers in Far West?" inquired the "Mormon."

"We want three men from your city," insolently and boldly answered the other. "We want Joseph Smith, Hyrum Smith and Sidney Rigdon, then we will burn your town to ashes and as the flames leap up we'll massacre and murder all we find within the city limits. That's what we want and intend."

The "Mormon" messenger, Col. Hinkle by name, grew pale at these words.

"Can we not devise some other way? Would you murder all? Let the innocent suffer as well as those whom you call guilty? Have mercy on us."

The other seeing the evident fear and treachery of the base colonel, proposed that if he could devise means to get the leaders of the Church into the mobbers' camp, to get all the "Mormons'" property that it might be divided among their enemies, and to give up all the arms and ammunition in the town, in return the rest of the Saints should be permitted to leave the state and be protected by the militia.

To this infamous proposal the traitor consented and returned to the town to comply with the conditions.

The night before this was spent by Lydia, in common with the rest of the women, in trying to place her household effects where they would not be destroyed in case the mob should fire the city.

"My dear," said the husband, "be careful of our little ones to-night, I must go out and join my brethren who are on guard. You will not be afraid will you?"

"Newel, God rules!" replied the dauntless woman.

As night came on, two brethren who were among those that had gone up to Crooked river came to the door, and asked Lydia if she could not find a hiding-place for them, saying that the mob were doubly enraged at those who were up at that fearful engagement and determined to murder every such man they could find.

One of them, James Emmet by name, was an old friend of Lydia's. She quietly told them that she would do all in her power to secrete them. Accordingly, the night was partly spent in making a little store-room adjoining the living-room as comfortable as possible for the two men. When daylight came the mother dressed her little ones and commenced her usual daily duties. She knew she was liable to be killed herself if these men were found in her house, but as she told her husband, so she comforted her heart now by saying, "God rules!"

CHAPTER VII

In the early morning of Wednesday, 31st of Oct., the flag of truce spoken of in the previous chapter was sent out, and the traitor soon returned to consummate his horrible plan.

The day was spent by the anxious mother in work and prayer. Often she bent her knees in humble petition for the safety of her children and the brethren concealed in her house that they might not be found.

Newel was away with the men who were trying to devise means to protect their homes and families.

In the afternoon a neighbor came in to say, "Joseph has gone out to the enemies' camp."

"God protect him!" replied Lydia.

"They, that is the Prophet, Brothers Rigdon and Pratt, Col. Wight and Brother Robinson, have gone along with Col. Hinkle to see if something can't be done to prevent the carrying out of the exterminating order sent by Governor Boggs."

"What exterminating order?"

"Why didn't you hear that Governor Boggs, you remember the rascal, the one who headed the mob in Jackson Co., had sent an order to this host of robbers outside the town, telling them that they are to wipe out every one of us? Giving them authority as an organized millitia. Well you must have staid close at home last night not to have heard that!"

"Yes," said Lydia, "I was very busy all night."

"So were we all! I am told that Major-general Wallack and General Doniphan were ordered to raise a thousand men and join this General Clark who has command of the whole, and this precious trio are now trying to make arrangements to murder us all in cold blood! This is indeed a land of freedom! Why, Sister Knight, I feel just as though my blood was boiling oil when I think of this inhuman outrage."

"Be calm, sister, let your heart rather be filled with humblest prayer, that God will turn aside their wicked purposes."

The indignant neighbor departed, with many wishes that "God would exterminate them root and branch if they did not speedily repent."

Not long after the woman had gone, the air was filled by shouts and hideous sounds from the mobbers' camp. Looking anxiously from the window, Lydia saw her husband hurrying to the house. On entering he cried,

"Lydia, Lydia, pray as you never prayed before. Our beloved Prophet is taken prisoner! The wretch who decoyed him out has betray his Prophet, his religion and his God! Listen to those awful sounds! May the God of Israel hold their lives as in His hand. My wife, these are bitter days."

"Newel, I am full of weakness."

"Do not go outside the house, for prowlers are around and will injure you if they find you in their power. I must go now, my girl. You know my very soul is bowed with prayer to God to preserve my wife and babes. Be brave as you always are, and I will come when I can and bring you word of what transpires."

"Be careful, my husband, and I feel that we shall be protected."

Once more the woman was left alone with her little ones and the brethren under her care. God and her own heart alone know the anxieties of the next few hours. But into her soul crept and brooded the sweet spirit that whispered to the troubled waves, "Be still." And she was calm. Oh, that awful night! Over every thing, into every house, down into the low places, high over the tree-tops sounded the piercing, shrieking yells of that blood-thirsty mob. The flesh would creep at the fiendish sounds, the heart would quiver with the fearful though that Joseph, the beloved one, was in their power. Ten thousand wolves could never make a sound so hideously inhuman, or so fiendishly triumphant as the yells and shouts that unceasingly arose from the throats of that murderous throng from evening shades till morning light. Were these men human? Oh yes. Were they civilized beings? Oh yes; there were seventeen ministers and nineteen commissioned officers, who led the mob.

The night was spent by Lydia in one long, anxious prayer. The next morning, the 1st of November, dawned cool and bright.

With the morning came Newel. He brought the sad news that the Patriarch and Brother Amasa Lyman were taken prisoners and removed to the enemy's camp.

"Newel, how will this end? My heart is torn with anxious fears, and yet the Spirit tells me all will yet be well."

"God grant it, Lydia," replied her husband. "What is the meaning of all this? Look from the window! Here is an army marching upon us. Good by and God protect you, I must go, for there is the signal for us to gather at the public square."

So saying, he hastily snatched his rifle from the wall and rushed to the square, where the signal drum was beating long and loud. On arriving there he was commanded by Gen. Lucas to give up his arms.

He replied, "Sir, my rifle is my own private property, no one has a right to demand it from me."

"Lay down your arms, you rascal, or I will have you shot."

Full of righteous indignation, the helpless man complied, seeing that many of his brethren were also disarmed.

Their leaders were gone but they were true Saints. And were they not also free-born American citizens?

As the men rushed into the public square they were all forced to obey the summary command "Give up your arms!"

When all were assembled, they were compelled at the point of the bayonet to sign a deed of trust of all their (the "Mormons'") possessions to Gen. Lucas to defray the expenses of this unholy war.

This unrighteous deed being accomplished, and all the men of the town being placed under guard, the mob swarmed out into the town, pillaging, foraging, insulting women and abusing little children. Stock were shot down and left on the streets to rot. Fields were destroyed, houses were searched, everything of any value was taken and any one who dared to remonstrate was brutally threatened with murder.

Every house was searched for the men who were at the tragedy of Crooked river. At last three ruffians came to Lydia's door, and one who seemed to be the leader asked: "Have you any men in the house?"

"You have our men under guard," answered the fearless woman.

"Have you any man in the house?"

"I tell you, my husband is on the public square a prisoner."

"Have you any arms in the house?"

"My husband took his rifle with him."

The little children seeing the ferocious men, were frightened and commenced to cry.

"Sir, go away from here, do you not see how frightened my little ones are?"

"Well, have you no men or arms in the house?"

"I tell you again my husband is a prisoner on the square, and he took his rifle with him."

"Upon my word, at least you've got plenty of Mormon blood and to spare."

So abruptly speaking he turned away and they all left the house, leaving the brave but trembling woman whispering to her children, "God rules!"

The next morning, the sun arose on a scene of desolation. Hundreds of houseless, homeless beings huddled together as best they could, weeping, sorrowing and sad, but peaceful and full of the testimony that all suffering was in Christ Jesus, and He would be their helper and comforter. Many were without food to eat, but those who had some, shared with those who had not.

The Prophets and leaders were gone, but ways must be devised to get out of the state. Only a few short months were given them in which to leave their desolate homes and corn-fields.

That day the leaders came into the town heavily guarded, and were marched to the square. There they were permitted, after much pleading, to see their distracted families. It was ascertained from the Prophet that a court-martial had been held, and the prisoners were tried without being allowed to be present or to have any one to defend them, and were sentenced to be shot the next day. Gen. Doniphan, who was a lawyer, told the mob he would have nothing do do with such unlawful high-handed proceedings, and in disgust left them, ordering all of his men to take up their march homeward.

This circumstance made the robbers hesitate, and accordingly it was determined to remove the prisoners to Independence.

Not long were they permitted to be with their friends, but were taken back to camp. The next morning the Prophet and Patriarch, Sidney Rigdon, P. P. Pratt, Lyman Wight, Amasa Lyman and George W. Robinson were started off for Independence.

CHAPTER VIII

Newel set to work to try and assist the homeless ones and feed the poor. To this labor he devoted himself through the Winter.

In February he determined to go, with the rest of his brethren who were leaving the State, but did not know how it could be accomplished.

"Lydia, how are we to manage?

"The mob have killed all my stock but one cow, and we can't very well ride her, or drive her alone."

"Can you not make some turn with the cow so that some one will move us?"

"Perhaps! At least I can try."

After a time a man was found who consented to take them to the Mississippi river for the cow. Accordingly hasty preparations were made, and in the cold Winter, the snow piled up, sometimes to the hubs of the wagon, the husband took his wife and children a journey of two hundred miles.

The snow was scraped away to make their beds, and the cold was ofttimes intense.

Detained through unavoidable circumstances at a small place called Huntsville, they did not reach the river until the first part of May, crossing it and reaching the other side poor, destitute, but oh, so grateful to be once more free! Free to rest from travel and hardships! Free to lie down, and to rise up with their hearts and mouths full of God's praises! Free to live as their conscience prompted them, without the fear of mobs or persecutions!

Once across the river, a low marshy plain covered with grass, stretched away for miles and miles. Here and there a few belts of timber served to relieve the monotony of the landscape, and down swept the waters of the king of American rivers. This was the sight that greeted the weary eyes of our travelers. A small settlement had been started at this place, on the river bank, but the settlers soon deserted it for its unhealthiness was too great to admit of any one living here in comfort for any length of time. One or two empty deserted houses stood here and there, and were soon taken possession of by the first comers.

Our friends, like many others, camped out. They made themselves as comfortable as possible by sewing some of their bed-clothing and the wagon-cover together, thus forming a rude tent.

What a picture this first settling of the place afterwards called Nauvoo must have been! A few houses scattered about, and everywhere tents, bush wickeups and rude shelters of every description dotting the grassy plain. The grass was green, but damp and moist. The water was plentiful and clear, but warm, and over all brooded the wings of the fatal miasma. One by one the families who had been driven from their peaceful homes, found their way across the river and settled here in peace.

Brigham Young had taken charge of this moving host, and the poor were all carefully provided for and moved, through the indomitable energies of Brother Brigham. Joseph was still a prisoner, and so all this responsibility devolved upon the president of the Twelve. History and the grateful hearts of the Saints will testify how well that charge was executed.

A few weeks served to show the people how deadly was the air arising from the swamps and marshes around about.

The sick, infirm and aged were the first victims of the foul miasma. Then little children were prostrated.

Fevers of all kinds contracted in malarious countries were very prevalent. Great numbers of the strong—men and women who had borne every hardship without flinching, lay down in their beds and succumbed to the terrible disease. Ague dragged his shivering, shaking length from door to door, and there were not sufficient strong ones left to bury the dead. Specters instead of men crept slowly about laying those who were sleeping the last sleep in their dreary graves. Pestilence and fever were seated at every fireside. Even Joseph who had escaped from his enemies and came to Nauvoo, soon lay prostrate in his house, and even his yard was filled with the sick, the dying and the dead.

At last the spirit of the invincible Prophet rallied from this blow, and rising up by the power of God he commenced going about healing the sick. Hundreds were so healed; and as the brethren were healed they would arise and follow the Prophet continuing the glorious work. There was a change from this very day. The general health of the people began to improve.

Lydia had managed to wait upon her own ailing child and those of her neighbors who were the most helpless, notwithstanding her health was far from being good. Pale and weak she ministered unto those around her until

September, when, worn out with her heavy labors and her body weakened by over-exertion, disease fastened itself upon her and she was prostrated.

For several days and nights she lay in a raging, burning fever, until it almost seemed as though her very flesh would be consumed upon her bones.

One day she called her husband to her bed and said:

"Newel, go and ask the Prophet to send me a handkerchief with his blessing."

"My dear wife, I do not like to trouble Joseph. You have no idea how worn down he is. He has asked the brethren to spare him as much as possible, for these constant never-ceasing calls upon him are depriving him of all his strength. I hope, my dear, you will soon be better."

The night came and passed and morning brought no relief to the weary sufferer.

Again she called Newel to her and entreated him to go to the Prophet and get a handkerchief with his blessing.

Newel went out, and in about half an hour returned, tied a handkerchief over her head saying:

"There, Lydia, is a handkerchief."

The sufferer experienced no relief from it, however, and rapidly grew worse.

A doctor was brought to her, and he tried his best to rally her, but all in vain. Thus one week passed.

One day Newel, seeing she was all but gone and was trying to speak to him, bent over her to catch the faint whisper,

"Newel, I am all but done with my suffering; good-by, dear one. You must do the best you can with the children. I cannot last much longer."

This was very brokenly whispered to the distracted man above her, who, as soon as she ceased, hurried away. Coming back soon, he called her; she knew him but was unable to reply.

"Here, Lydia, here is a handkerchief from the Prophet Joseph. Oh my wife, the one I brought before was not from him, I so hated to trouble him. But see this is from Joseph, and he says your Heavenly Father shall heal you, and you shall be restored to life and health."

The handkerchief was bound around her brow, and as it touched her head, the blessing sent with it, descended upon her; and over her and all through her was poured the spirit of healing. Sleep, so long a stranger to the poor afflicted one, closed her eye-lids in a quiet, restful, blessed slumber.

The hours came and fled, and in the quiet of midnight she awoke, and was like one who had been in a dark, loathsome dungeon, and was again free in the open air and sunshine. In the morning the physician came, and when he saw his patient, he exclaimed:

"Why, I never saw such a change in my life! That last medicine has worked like a charm, I wish I'd stayed and seen it operate. Her pulse is all right, her tongue is all right, and in fact she is comparatively a well woman."

After the docter had praised up himself and his medicine to his heart's content, Newel quietly reached the bottle down from the shelf, and said:

"Sir, there is the medicine you speak of. My wife has not tasted one drop of it."

"But what's the meaning of all this change then?"

"She has been healed by faith through the Prophet Joseph Smith."

After studying some time over the matter the docter said:

"Well it's a good thing to get well on any terms."

The good docter soon after departed, as he plainly saw his services were no longer needed. He was not a "Mormon," although a kind, worthy man.

That day Lydia arose and dressed herself, and went forth to her daily cares.

She found her oldest boy, Samuel, well, and full of a desire to help all he could. The little fellow would take his tiny pail and go to the river, thus supplying the family with all the water needed.

This was in the fall of '39, and her little girl was three years old. She also was well and trotting about the house at her baby plays. The babe James, was very ill. Fever had reduced him to a skeleton, and the mother's heart ached as she looked at his wasted body; but not once did she think of his dying.

Newel was also stricken down after this, and a young girl, Newel's niece, Harriet, who lived with them.

From one to the other went Lydia giving simple remedies, praying for them and doing all in her power to relieve their sufferings.

Once in a while the neighbors would come in and try to help her all they could, although they had their own sick ones at home to attend. Whenever they did come, they would say to her:

"Sister Knight, you can not keep that child; why do you cling so to him? You will displease our Father. Let him go, give him up, and his sufferings will be at an end."

"Oh I cannot think of such a thing!" replied the quiet woman. "Father Smith said in my blessing that my heart should not be pained because of the loss of my children. And I cannot, let him go because I feel that it is not the Lord's will that I should part with him."

On the Sunday following this, the child lay like a breathing skeleton. The skin drawn, the eyes glassy and the breath all but stopped.

The mother knelt over him in an agony of watchfulness.

"Oh Newel, what shall I do? He is sinking so fast. Tell me, advise me! I must do something, or he cannot live!"

The husband looked sadly from the sick bed where he lay, at his little child, but with more sorrow in his eyes for his distracted wife, and at last said:

"You can do no more. Give him up and ask God to soften this great blow to us both."

"Give him up," cried the mother, "give up my boy to the arms of the destroyer! It is impossible. I *cannot* give him up."

With burning eyes, but a determined heart she watched him through the long, silent hours of the night. The next morning early, the Prophet chanced to pass the house and Lydia ran out and asked him to come in and see her little child who was nigh unto death. He came in and going up to the child he was shocked at his appearance.

"He is sick indeed. I will tell you one thing more to do, and if that does not save him, you will have to give him up."

"I cannot give him up," the woman replied.

Joseph looked at her, into her clear, calm, determined eyes, and over his face came a peculiar heavenly smile, a smile that was so glorious in its meaning, and said:

"Sister Lydia, I do not think you will have to give him up."

Then, after a moment's thought, "you must send for Father Geo. W. Harris; take some warm water and soap, wash your child from the crown of his head to the soles of his feet; then have Father Harris annoint him with holy consecrated oil from the crown of his head to the soles of his feet; and I think your child will live."

Lydia lost no time in obeying his words, and when the blessing was over she had the joy of seeing her child revive and he was healed.

On Thursday morning after, Joseph came in to see how the child was, and was pleased to find him restored to health.

"Now, Sister Lydia," he remarked as he was going away, "should your babe take a relapse, you know what has healed it before, do the same again."

That evening, the disease seemed to return and fasten itself closer than ever on the frail child.

Lydia immediately sent for Brother Harris, but he was away from home. The night was again spent in anxious watching.

In the morning she called in two brethren, and she and they repealed the former ceremony of washing and annointing the babe. As the brethrens' hands rested upon his head, a light shone down upon him, like a brilliant sunbeam from a cloudy sky. "The light" faded as they ceased, and the child was completely restored to health from that moment.

CHAPTER IX

The Autumn and Winter passed pleasantly away. Health being restored, homes were being being made for these tent-dwellers.

The busy hum of the workman sounded on every side. Trees were set out; houses, one-roomed, two-roomed and sometimes double-storied, slowly arose to take the place of the parti-colored tents.

The first time Joseph came across Newel, he shook hands with him and enquired:

"Have you brought your mill?"

"No, sir; I had no way to move my mill, it was much too heavy to bring."

"Well now, Brother Newel, I want to give you a mission. Grain is very plentiful here; flour and meal are scarce as it is so far to the nearest mill. Now, go to; build a mill and accomplish it as soon as possible."

This was in the first Spring that they were there, in '39. Brother Knight spent the Summer in erecting a mill. After it was completed he was taken ill, as was related in the last Chapter. On his recovery, he set to work to build a log cabin for his family.

Lydia took possession of her new house as proud as any queen, and far happier.

In October, on the eighteenth of the month, 1840, a little son came to Newel and Lydia, whom they called Joseph, after his grandfather. Two years passed happily and busily away, and on the 14th of October, 1842, another son came to their home, he was called after his father, Newel. The house, its care, the duties of a mother and wife occupied the hands and mind of Lydia during this time.

In 1842, the Relief Society was formed by the Prophet Joseph. It was an organization of women for the relief of the poor, the culture and improvement of its members. Joseph, in organizing it stated that the Church of God would not be complete without this society.

Sister Lydia was enrolled as one of its first members.

The years of '42 and '43, passed away. During this time the Prophet was eagerly sought for by his enemies. Again and again was he taken prisoner for imaginary offenses, and once some ruffians tried to kidnap him into Missouri.

In the Spring of '44, persecution raged high against the leaders of the Church. Mobs once more began to gather and commit depredations.

In the midst of all these persecutions and tribulations a little girl was born to Lydia, on the 6th of June, 1844.

As she began to recover her strength a little, rumors that the blood-hounds were again seeking the life of the Prophet grew more and more frequent. On the 24th of June, Joseph gave himself up to his enemies, his brother Hyrum and eighteen others going with him.

The narrative of the horrible, sickening murder of the Prophet and Patriarch which occurred on the 27th is too ghastly in its details to give in this little story. Who can tell the bitter anguish, the wild unavailing woe that struck the faithful hearts of the Saints in Nauvoo!

The murdered Prophet and Patriarch were brought back to Nauvoo for burial, but Lydia was too weak and too much overcome with grief to attend the services over their remains.

Mourning, deep and solemn, filled the city. And every heart was wrung with grief and woe. But over all brooded the spirit of Christ.

Time passed on without anything of special moment occurring to Lydia or family until the Summer of '45. The Winter of '45, however, brought two little orphan girls to her care by the name of Ames. From the time that Lydia had her first home in Missouri, it might almost be said until the present, her home has been the peaceful asylum for some one or two children who have been homeless.

In the summer of '45, just a year, a month and a day from the time of the martyrs' death. Newel and his wife paid a visit to the scene of the murder.

The jailor's wife who admitted them, showed them up stairs to the large, low-ceilinged room where the deed was committed.

"Do you know," the loquacious woman said, as she lifted the carpets up from the floor, "I have scoured and scrubbed those spots with all my might and it's no manner of use; just as soon as the water is dried off they are as bright as they were the first day. And look at these scars in the wall," the woman seemed to be possessed, as she spoke, with a trembling horror, "I have tried my best to get them filled up."

"Can't they be leveled up? I should think a good plasterer could fill them up," observed Mr. Knight as he examined the holes in the plaster evidently made by rifle and pistol balls.

"Well, you would think so perhaps; but the best workmen in the country have endeavored to plaster the scars up, and you see them now as plain as they were a year ago. The plasterer no sooner leaves his job, than next morning it is all to do over again. It was a terrible affair."

Too much overcome by the remembrance of the tragedy committed there to answer the woman or remain longer on the spot. Newel and Lydia hastily left and wended their way homeward with heavy hearts.

About this time the wicked and those who wished the destruction of "Mormonism," grew more bold and committed depredations without number.

The Saints who were so unfortunate as to live outside the confines of Nauvoo, were annoyed, abused, insulted and maltreated. People began to move into Nauvoo as the mob became fiercer and stronger; for houses and barns were burned, and all the awful scenes of rapine and pillage of Far West and Jackson county were repeated with redoubled violence.

No law could be found strong enough to reach these robbers; no official just enough to punish the perpetrators of the crimes which were constantly committed.

Lydia often looked around her little home and wondered if she would again be driven from all her comforts. One evening Newel came home from council where he had been for hours, with a very sad face.

"Well, dear, what is to be done? Why are you so downcast?"

"Reason enough, my girl. Brother Brigham and the council have decided that we must once more turn our faces westward, and again flee into the wilderness. The outrages of the mob have become so frequent, and they are so encouraged in their deviltry by those who should protect us, that our leaders have given the word to take up the line of march."

"If it be so, Newel, it will ill become us to murmur or indulge in useless regrets. Our place is with the kingdom of God. Let us at once set about making preparations to leave."

The Winter of '46 was spent by most of the Saints in laboring in the temple. As soon as it became generally known that another exodus was to be made, all who were able devoted their time to receiving their blessings in the house of God.

As Spring came on Lydia grew anxious to start on the proposed long journey. Many of the Saints had left or were leaving, and at last Newel succeeded in getting two wretched wagons, three yoke of oxen and one or two cows. A few necessary utensils and the provisions for three months were packed in one wagon, and the family in the other. Thus equipped Newel and Lydia joined a moving company and left Nauvoo on the morning of the 17th of April, 1846. They left mills, house, barn and all their possessions to be occupied by any of the mobbers who might chance to come first.

What a journey! For hundreds and hundreds of miles after leaving Nauvoo stretched away an unbroken prairie. How very long seemed a mile when traversed by oxen! Often the wheels of the wagons would be up to the hubs in the soft, miry land. But here, at least, was freedom. In the evenings the great camp-fires were lit, supper was cooked on the glowing coals and the little ones were put quietly to sleep. Then a merry, cheerful crowd collected around the fire, and talked of the prospects for making homes where mobs could not come. About nine o'clock the little circle would kneel down in simple, humble worship to the Great Omnipotent, and then retire to rest.

The Sundays were always days of rest. A temporary halt was made, and meetings were held. Oh the peace, the rest of those quiet Sabbath days! How fervently Lydia sang,

"Praise God from whom all blessings flow!" How her heart swelled with love to Him who had brought her to these lovely, quiet days!

Four weeks' travel and the company arrived at Mount Pisgah, where they found many of the Saints who were resting and recruiting their teams.

Two or three weeks were spent here. Then again the march was taken up, and again the untrodden prairie rolled away as far as the eye could reach.

Two weeks of slow traveling brought the company to Council Bluffs, where another halt for rest and recuperation was made.

The provisions in Brother Knight's wagon had become very low, and so Newel went down into Missouri and got a few jobs of work that gave him the means to get another stock of food; this time he got ample provisions for one year.

One month had passed, and the word was given to start. The "Mormons" built a ferry-boat and crossed the Missouri river. The company were then all drawn up on a pleasant camping place and here they awaited the arrival of Presidents Brigham Young, Heber C. Kimball and Willard Richards, who were coming to regularly organize the company.

In a few days the Presidency arrived. President Young had sent a call to all who could furnish themselves with a year's provisions, and a team able to travel, to cross the river and await his coming. Here then they were, and prepared for the organization, which took place on the same day as he arrived.

"My brethren," said the President, "I am pleased to see you so well equipped. We shall organize you into companies of fifty. That is, fifty families in one company, the charge of which shall be given to a captain. You will then be further divided into companies of tens, also presided over by captains. This will insure order and good, careful management. It is imperatively necessary that the utmost unity should prevail. Let every one be careful to cultivate the spirit of obedience to those who will be placed to direct. The journey you are to pursue is one of many dangers and difficulties. You are about to enter into a wilderness where the foot of white man has never pressed the earth. Be prudent! Let not the women venture far from the camp. Keep the strictest watch over the little children that they do not stray. Be careful in all that you do. God will surely watch over you, but you must also exert your utmost vigilance. Never anger the Indians by whom you may be surrounded, but follow the dictates of the Spirit which will lead you to act wisely and cautiously. Let no man set up his judgment against your captain, lest disunion creep in among you, and you shall be deserted by the good Spirit. Be watchful, be obedient and be prudent and you shall be preserved from evil, from the Indians, from the power of the destroyer, and harm of every kind inasmuch as you pay heed to my counsels. You are to go on until you reach the Rocky Mountains, or until you find good wintering for yourselves and stock. I will appoint Newel Knight to take the charge of the first company of fifty, and Joseph Holbrook to be captain of the second company of fifty. These brethren are to have control of the camps, and God will do unto you all even as you keep the commandments He has given you and the counsel I have just given."

Brothers Kimball and Richards also left many blessings with this little party who formed the first organized company for overland travel. Soon after the departure of the Presidency, the emigrating Saints again set out, slowly traveling by day and quietly resting by night.

A week thus spent and they were overtaken by a company under Jas. Emmet and George Miller, who had set up jointly to take the lead of the Church. They had gathered up a company in Missouri and were determined to be ahead in the grand exodus. These men immediately attempted to assume command of the two companies under Brothers Knight and Holbrook.

I must explain this circumstance thoroughly as its bearing on what followed is very important:

There was much discussion, and Newel maintained that he had not been instructed by Brother Brigham to submit to the authority of either Emmet or Miller.

Two weeks were spent in argument and remonstrance, all traveling on, until when within six miles of the missionary station of the Pawnee Indians. By this time quite a number had been so impressed with the perilous picture drawn by Miller and Emmet of their course if they did not unite with his company, that there was quite a division in the camp. A council of the officers was held, and it was decided that Newel Knight and John Kay should return to Winter Quarters, where the body of the Saints were encamped for Winter, and there obtain the word and will of the Lord through His servant Brigham.

Only a short time elapsed before the messengers who were sent to Winter Quarters returned with a letter from President Young. He counseled them not to attempt to reach the mountains, as the season was now to far advanced. But to seek some good place, where people and teams could be fed and be made comfortable through the Winter. And thus it was, the three companies united, and, for the time at least, Emmet and Miller submitted to counsel. The captains then sought for a suitable place to winter.

Some Ponca Indian chiefs came up while the party were in doubt what to do, and after learning what the white men wished, offered them a Winter asylum on their lands. They said, only a few suns would bring them over to the place, and that there were grass and water in abundance.

Accordingly, the companies made their slow way across the plains, traveling two wrecks over the place the swift Indian ponies had traversed in two or three days.

The red men were very kind and hospitable to the white men. Many of them had never before seen a pale-face; and the wagons, cattle, pigs, sheep and chickens were objects of wonder and admiration. The white men were equally amused with the odd dress, manners and habits of the children of the prairie.

A treaty was made for mutual interest and protection, and as Winter drew on, the little camp were getting very comfortable, with log cabins for homes and stables.

Lydia was calm and happy, and looked forward to the time when the end of the long journey would be reached, and she and Newel were once again settled in a home with the dear little ones growing up around them.

The Winter had nearly spent its violence, when over the little cabin where Lydia worked and hoped there was cast a lingering shadow. A shadow dark and grim.

One night in the beginning of January, the shadow drifted in and silently settled down on the faithful husband. She did not see its dusky wings as Newel's voice awoke her, but dimly, so dimly wondered what strange influence was in the room. The grip of the shadowy presence was fastened on Newel, and he knew it.

"Lydia, I have a pain in my side. Be quick, my dear, it is very acute."

The remedy was brought but gave no relief.

On the 11th of January, a woman sat with tightly-closed hands and wild agonized eyes watching the breath of the being she loved better than life itself, slowly cease.

"Lydia," the dying voice faintly whispered, "it is necessary for me to go. Joseph wants me. It is needful that a messenger be sent with the true condition of the Saints. Don't grieve too much, for you will be protected."

"Oh Newel, don't speak so; don't give up; oh I could not bear it. Think of me. Newel, here in an Indian country alone, with seven little children. No resting place for my feet, no one to counsel, to guide, or to protect me. I cannot let you go."

The dying man looked at her a moment, and then said with a peculiar look: "I will not leave you now Lydia."

As the words left his lips, an agony of suffering seemed to seize him. His very frame trembled with the mighty throes of pain.

The distracted wife bore his agony as long as she could, but at last, flinging herself on her knees, she cried to God to forgive her if she had asked amiss, and if it was really His will for her husband to die, that the pain might leave him and his spirit go in peace.

The prayer was scarcely over ere a calm settled on the sufferer, and with one long loving look in the eyes of his beloved wife, the shadow lifted and the spirit fled.

CHAPTER X

Alone in an Indian country, uncertain where she would go or what she should do, this woman with seven little helpless children took up the burden of life. In and through her surged the consciousness that God doeth all things well. But oh the awful, the silent loneliness!

That evening (11th of Jan.), Newel was buried. No lumber could be had, so Lydia had one of her wagon-boxes made into a rude coffin. The day was excessively cold, and some of the brethren had their fingers and feet frozen while digging the grave and performing the last offices of love for their honored captain and brother.

As the woman looked out upon the wilderness of snow and saw the men bearing away all that was left of her husband, it seemed that the flavor of life had fled and left only dregs, bitter unavailing sorrow. But as she grew calmer she whispered with poor, pale lips, "God rules!"

Time was empty of incident or interest to Lydia until the 4th of February, when Brother Miller, who had been to Winter Quarters for provisions, returned, and brought tidings of a revelation showing the order of the organization of the camp of the Saints, and also the joyful news that Brothers E. T. Benson and Erastus Snow were coming soon to Ponca to organize the Saints according to the pattern given in the revelation.

On the day of the organization, Lydia returned from the meeting and sat down in her home full of sad thoughts. How could she, who had never taken any care except that which falls to every woman's share, prepare herself and family to return to Winter Quarters and from thence take a journey of a thousand miles into the Rocky Mountains. The burden weighed her very spirit down until she cried out in her pain: "Oh Newel, why hast thou left me!"

As she spoke, he stood by her side, with a lovely smile on his face, and said: "Be calm, let not sorrow overcome you. It was necessary that I should go. I was needed behind the vail to represent the true condition of this camp and people. You cannot fully comprehend it now; but the time will come when you shall know why I left you and our little ones. Therefore, dry up your tears. Be patient, I will go before you and protect you in your journeyings. And you and your little ones shall never perish for lack of food. Although the ravens of the valley should feed you and your little ones you shall not perish for the want of bread."

As he spoke the last words, she turned, and there appeared three ravens. Turning again to where her husband had stood, he was not.

This was a great comfort and help to her, and her spirits were revived and strengthened by the promises made.

As spring began to approach, the little camp was visited a great deal by sickness and death.

The Sioux Indians ran off all the stock they could and generally were very troublesome.

March came, and Lydia's journal is filled with the little incidents of camp life, and on every page the over-burdened heart tells its own tale of sorrow and mourning.

In April, the word was given to move. The camp was organized for traveling and the Saints commenced their journey.

Lydia started out with her family and effects in two wagons drawn by three yoke of oxen, and driven by Samuel, who was thirteen years old and James who was nine.

The brethren were exceedingly kind to the widow and rendered her all the assistance in their power. There is no kindness on earth more freely bestowed than that given by the Saints to those who are in trouble.

A very cold, slow, tedious journey was made down to Winter Quarters. Arriving there, or nearly there, the camp split up and scattered as sheep without a shepherd, thus disregarding President Young's counsel, who wished them to remain at a certain location two miles from the town. Those who were able, fitted up to go on to the valley with the companies moving there that Spring, while about ten families under Captain David Lewis remained at the place designated by President Young, named afterwards Ponca Camp.

One year was spent by Lydia in this place. Almost immediately after she reached Ponca Camp, she was counseled to send her step-son, Samuel, on to the valley. Although she did so, she feared lest his mother's relatives might take the boy away from her, and she felt she could not bear to lose him, for he was almost as dear to her as her own sons.

The brethren put up a log cabin for her, and with the help of the nine year old son, she raised plenty of vegetables through the Summer. Her cows did well, and she was very comfortable.

On the 26th of August, a little boy was born to Lydia. She had just moved into the cabin, in which there were no doors nor windows and the roof was but partially on. However, she and the child did well.

When the little babe was a week old, a sudden severe rain-storm came up. It poured down into the cabin with much violence. Lydia told her daughter Sally to give her all the bed-clothes they had, and these were put upon the bed and removed as they became soaked:

At last, finding the clothes were all wet completely through and that she was getting chilled sitting up in the wet, she said: "Sally, go to bed, it's no use doing any more unless some power beyond that which we possess is exercised, it is impossible for me to avoid catching cold. But we will trust in God, He has never failed to hear our prayers."

And so she drew her babe to her, and covered up as well as she could, and asked God to watch over them all through the night.

Her mind went back to the time when she had a noble companion, one who would never allow her to suffer any discomfort, and who loved her as tenderly as man could woman. But now he was in the grave in a savage Indian country, and she was alone and in trouble.

As she thus mused, chilled with the cold rain and shivering, her agony at his loss became unbearable and she cried out: "Oh Newel, why could you not have stayed with and protected me through our journeyings?"

A voice plainly answered her from the darkness around her, and said: "Lydia, be patient and fear not. I will still watch over you, and protect you in your present situation. You shall receive no harm. It was needful that I should go, and you will understand why in due time."

As the voice ceased, a pleasant warmth crept over her, and seemed like the mild sunshine on a lovely Spring afternoon.

Curling down in this comfortable atmosphere, she went immediately to sleep, and awoke in the morning all right, but wet to the skin.

Instead of receiving harm from this circumstance, she got up the next morning, although the child was but a week old, and went about her usual labors.

In the Spring, the Indians came down in great numbers. Winter Quarters was vacated by the Saints, who moved across the river to Pottowattamie. This removal was caused by the jealousy of the Indians, who wished them to get away from the land on which was built Winter Quarters, as it was part of their reservation.

The Ponca Camp was advised by President Young to move into Pottowattamie, as the Indians were troublesome, or apt to be so, at this place also. Accordingly, a general move was made across the river.

President Young, who had been to the valley the year before, returned now to remove his family. The word was given for all that could, to fit out and go with the President; those who could not, were to go to Pottowattamie, and there remain until either they were able to move or the Church could assist them to do so.

Lydia had at this time two wagons, three yoke of oxen and three cows. She went over to Winter Quarters on the 30th of April, '48, to ask President Young's counsel as to her going west with the company.

After representing her condition to him, the President replied: "Sister Knight, you have a large family of helpless children, and all who go to the valley must provide themselves with at least eighteen months' provisions. With your teams, it would be impossible to haul half that, and it would be the cause of suffering for yourself and little ones to be in the valley unless you have plenty to last. You know, of course, we must raise our crops before we can expect to have anything, and there is nothing but seed crops in this Spring. Now sister, you will be much more comfortable to go over to Pottowattamie and stay there until you can come, and find something to come to. If you feel so disposed, you can let your three yoke of oxen and two wagons go towards helping to fit out some one who can go and take care of themselves when there."

His words reminded Lydia of a covenant her husband, in common with the faithful Elders, had made in Nauvoo, that they and all they possessed should be upon the altar for the assistance of those to remove to the valley who were otherwise unable to get there, and that they would never cease their exertions until the removal was made.

Was not this covenant hers?

Without a moment's hesitation, she replied: "Certainly, President Young, they are at your disposal."

She then returned to her home in Ponca Camp and prepared to go across the river.

The camp and Winter Quarters were situated on the west side of the Missouri, and Pottowattamie was on the east side. It was thought best for Sister Knight to leave her teams and wagons on the west side, and some of the brethren assisted her across, thus avoiding much ferrying, which was expensive and troublesome as so many were crossing backwards and forwards.

Arriving on the east side, she found herself in Pottowattamie again without a roof to shelter her head.

After some search, a Doctor Lee, who had moved her across the river, found her a sort of half-cave, half-hut on the bank of a creek. The sides were of logs, the back being the side of the hill against which it was built. This was one of the most miserable habitations in which a human being ever lived. Cold in Winter, sultry in the Summer, filthy and low. However, Lydia lived here one year.

In the Spring of '49, the waters as usual rose very high. One afternoon, Lydia took her pail to get some water from the swollen stream running by the door. As she reached the bank, she saw her little girl's head on the top of the water as she was floating down the stream. Dashing in she grasped the child, and, after some severe struggles, succeeded in reaching the bank with the almost drowned child. After several hours rubbing, and administering to the child, she recovered, and only a mother could imagine Lydia's joy at her return to life.

The following extract from a letter written by Lydia to her parents, July 10th, 1848, shows the spirit of this quiet but energetic woman, who as a girl never left "till the last lock was pulled:"

"There are times when it seems as though every power were exerted to discourage me in what I believe to be the path of duty. And were it not that my confidence is in God and my faith firmly stayed upon the Mighty One of Jacob, I am sure I would shrink and fall beneath the burden that is upon me. I embraced the religion of the Latter-day Saints because my judgment was convinced that it was necessary for my salvation, and for this reason I now cling to it. * * * Contrary to my expectations when I last wrote, I have crossed the Missouri river. I have not yet been able to procure an outfit to take me to the valley, and I do not know when I can. It requires my whole time and attention to provide for the daily wants of myself and family. Yet amid my trials I am happy and feel assured that my Maker will provide for me, and in His own due time gather me with His people. * * * I trust that you, my dear parents, will at some future time be induced to cast your lot with the Saints. If this desire of my heart could be fulfilled I would experience a joy which words would fail to express. I still trust in God, knowing that He will do all things for the best."

CHAPTER XI

What sufferings must have been endured by these brave, faithful, single-hearted, pioneer "Mormon" women. Pen and tongue are weak to express the struggles and trials of these heroines of modern times.

Lydia was still in her little den into which she had moved when coming to the place one year ago; flooded when it rained, intensely cold in Winter, hot and stifling in the Summer, and always damp, low, unhealthy and impossible to make, or keep clean. Lydia was too neat and thrifty to tamely submit to such a state of things any longer than possible. She felt weak in her own spirit when alone with her sad thoughts, but when the occasion presented itself for action, she was prepared for it.

In June, she heard that the Widow Ensign was about to move to the valley, and wished to sell her cabin and a few acres of farming land. Accordingly she set out to see if she could purchase it. She had been washing and sewing for those of the Saints who could pay for such things, and had saved thereby a few dollars.

She offered the widow what money she had together with some clothing and household effects which she could ill spare, for her cabin and land. The offer was readily accepted, as it was not very easy to sell property, so many were constantly leaving for the valley.

Then, here was Lydia, without a dime and but very few personal effects, settling down for another year, with no prospect of reaching the Mecca of all her hopes, the valley, for at least another year. However, she had a tolerably decent log cabin, which possessed the merit of keeping out the rain, and which could be made a clean dwelling place for herself and little ones. She moved into her new home on the 23rd of June, and her devout spirit breathed a fervent prayer of gratitude to God, as she entered its portals, that she and her children were still alive and well, and that their surroundings were so much improved.

The children were now sent to school, and Lydia took in washing and other work to keep herself and family.

On the 30th of June she writes:

"Have been doing some washing for miners that I may get some money to buy meal. To-day I went with my son to the mill to get something to make bread for my family. Just as I was leaving, a gentleman, learning my situation, told the miller to put up twenty pounds of flour for me, at his expense. May the Lord reward him bountifully."

How many times in the history of this people have unknown friends aided them when in distress! Surely angels must have carefully watched over them in their manifold sufferings.

During harvest, the brethren "took hold" and harvested Lydia's wheat.

The Winter of '49-'50 was spent very peacefully by this patient woman. Her children, whom she had always taught at home previously, were now at school. Busy with her needle and wash-tub, to earn enough to feed and clothe her little ones, the time flew quickly by, and as Spring came on Lydia felt an almost irrepressible desire to make a start to emigrate to the valley.

"James," she said one day to her oldest son, "can't we make an effort to get to the valley this season?"

"Why, mother, what will you go with? President Young took our two teams and wagons and you know we only got back one team and part of the two wagons. What was the reason, mother, that the wagons were so broken up and almost fit for nothing?"

"Well, my son, I have heard it rumored that the teamsters in crossing the plains, returning here, as they did not have proper restraint and care over them, were a little foolish and perhaps cut up the more cumbersome parts of some wagons for firewood."

"How would they drive them?"

"They did not drive the broken wagons, my boy, but would load the more valuable part of several wagons, such as wheels, axle-trees, etc., yoke up long strings of oxen on this wagon, and thus save hunting up wood, or going without, where wood was scarce. But let us say nothing about it; we will be very thankful to have what is here. I have given the pieces of one wagon to get the other one repaired, so that we may have one good wagon. Bishop Hunter was here the other day; he has come on to bring a company of the poorer of the Saints, and will help them with the Emigration Fund, where they are unable to come any other way. Now, the kind Bishop tells me that President Young has given him especial charge to bring us out this season; and he offers me the use of two yoke of oxen. He says I can pay for their use when I get to the valley and earn enough to do so. This, of course, I will do as soon as I possibly can."

"Well, but mother, ain't we poor?"

"Yes, James, but God will always help those to be independent who earnestly desire to be so. We will be blessed in the future as we have been in the past."

It was thus decided to get ready to move westward with Bishop Hunter's company, and Lydia very rapidly completed her preparations for the long journey across the plains. Under Bishop Hunter's advice she sold, for a small sum of money, the yoke of oxen that had returned the previous year from the valley, and turned the proceeds into a little fund for the outfit.

A brother, named Grover, whom she had known in Kirtland, and had been friendly with all through the various moves of the Saints, hearing of her destitute circumstances, and that she was about to emigrate to the valley, came in one day and gave her twenty-five dollars in cash.

She also sold the little cabin and piece of land for about twenty dollars, receiving her pay in corn.

This corn was prepared for the journey in a very odd manner. The children spent many days in parching it; after which it was taken to the mill and ground up. This was done by the advice of President Young, in order to preserve the meal sweet and good. The greater part of the corn was thus prepared; but Lydia carried some meal unparched. She bought a sack of flour weighing one hundred pounds, and thus had for the journey about seven or eight hundred pounds of flour and meal together parched and unparched. A few pounds of dried fish, some soap, eight or ten pounds of sugar, a few matches and a little soda, formed the grocery stores. Her medicine chest consisted solely of a bottle of consecrated oil.

One pair of shoes and a stout, home-made suit or dress with a better one for Sunday use for each of the children; a good shawl for herself and warm wraps for the little ones, made up the scanty wardrobe. But she had quite a good supply of bedding which was of great service to her on the journey. A little stove was set up in the wagon to keep them warm, and a little rocking-chair in the front end of the wagon for Lydia to sit in, were among her selections for the trip. However, she soon found that even these supplies would not go in the wagon, and give room for the seven little ones. Although but twelve years of age, James walked most of the way to the valley and drove the oxen, while Joseph, Newel and Sally walked a great part of the way; but even then, a place must be found for the three smaller ones, beside the mother. So after talking the matter over a great deal, Lydia concluded to yoke up two of her cows on lead of one yoke of oxen, and put the odd cow and the other yoke of oxen on some wagon belonging to the company, the owner of which would allow her to have the use of part of the wagon for her share. Bro. Cluff offered to let Lydia put her cow and oxen on one of his wagons, and partly load the wagon with her things, he having one of his boys to drive. Bro. Cluff was pretty well off, had ten or twelve boys, and was well able to assist the widow.

Lydia found herself ready about the 1st of June, 1850, and started with Bro. Cluff 's folks, traveling as far as Salt River, and then halting for the rest of the company to come up. In about two weeks, the whole company was gathered, organized and ready to start. As was the custom, the party was divided into companies of one hundred; then subdivided into fifties, which were again divided into companies of ten. Bishop Hunter was the presiding captain, and Jesse Haven was the captain of the ten in which were Lydia and her friends, the Cluffs.

For many days they traveled upon the prairie, a level sea of waving green, without a mound or hill to rest the weary eye. After striking the Platte river, they followed it up for hundreds of miles. Sometimes they would reach a little grove of trees, sometimes some brush, or a little driftwood caught in a snag in the river. This was all the wood the camp ever found while on the prairie; and the prudent widow always carefully laid by some wood in her wagon to serve when there was none where they camped.

For very many miles the train moved along the plains up the Platte river, which were then called the "buffalo country." Often in the distance they would see herds of these creatures. One day, they were traveling in a little more hilly part of the country, and became aware that the hills were covered with thousands of these herds. What was thought at first to be trees, turned out to be a moving mass of buffalos; and upon the head wagons getting near enough to see, they found that some of these immense herds were crossing from the hills down to the river to water. A halt had to be called, and some hours were spent waiting for the road to be cleared for a passage.

It was here in this "buffalo country," that the famous stampedes of the animals were wont to take place. Without one second's warning, every ox and cow in the whole train would start to run, and go almost like a shot out of a gun. No matter how weary, or how stupid they were, when one made the spring, the remainder of the horned stock were crazed with fear. On, on, they would go for miles, and seemed unable to stop until headed and brought back to camp. One day while slowly plodding along beneath the burning, sultry sun, the start was made, and as every wagon was drawn by oxen or cows, away went cattle, wagons and inmates; tin and brass pails, camp-kettles and coffee-pots jingling merrily behind and underneath the wagons where they were tied; children screaming, everything that was loose flying out as they bumped along; over the untrodden prairie flew the maddened cattle, nearer and nearer to the river bank, which was here a precipice of twenty-five feet down to the water. Women, seeing their danger, sobbed out wild prayers for God to save; men ran and shouted to no avail; when suddenly over the plumy grass flies a horseman, spurring and screaming to his quivering, panting horse; mothers clasp their frightened babes in their arms, and prepare to face their watery grave. But the rider is up with the head team, and just as the head wagons are within ten feet of the deadly bank, he turns them aside and they are saved.

Lydia's wagon was near the lead, and she came within a few feet of the precipice. When she once more was safely traveling in the road, she and her children thanked God for His deliverance, praying that they might be so endangered no more. Her prayer was granted.

Another stampede occurred, but it was in the night and no one was hurt. The wagons, at night, were drawn up in a circle, the tongue of one resting upon the hind wheel of the preceding wagon; inside of this ring, the cattle were coralled. One night the camp heard the sudden start, and over one wagon over which the lead ox had leaped, went the whole herd. The wagon, which belonged to John Kay, was badly broken up. Out into the prairie ran the cattle; but as speedily as possible a man jumped on a horse, and riding furiously until he got ahead of the herd, he circled round and brought them back to camp. The cattle, when stampeding, always follow a leader, so the horseman took advantage of this, making a circle of some ten miles around to get back to camp.

From ten to twelve miles, was the average day's travel. At night, on reaching camp, the ring of wagons was formed, the cattle were turned out to feed, and then tents (by those who had them) were spread, camp-fires lit, supper cooked by the women; beds made in and under wagons, and in tents; supper eaten, and children put to bed. After dishes were washed and put away, the horn blew and the camp would gather in the center of the circle, a hymn would be sung, and prayer offered to God for future protection with thanksgiving for His past mercies.

Then the cattle would be brought up and corraled, and the older people would gather around the camp-fires; sometimes to sing, sometimes to tell stories of the past, and sometimes even to dance on the level space cleared for the purpose.

At daylight the cattle were again turned out to feed upon the grass, the horn blew, and singing and prayer were offered up to God. Breakfast was soon prepared and eaten, wagons packed, oxen yoked and the day's march was again taken up. No swearing, either at oxen or in any other way was allowed. No one was allowed to wander off; no running of teams, no team could try to pass another, no camp-fires must burn at night after retiring. Great care was taken that the prairies should not be set on fire.

Sabbath day, the train remained in camp, holding service and praising God, resting from the week's journey and toil.

Sometimes a halt would be made for a day or so that the women might wash and iron, and patch up the clothes. At such times, the young men would take their guns, getting permission from their various captains, and go out hunting; rabbits, deer and sometimes a buffalo would be the results of these expeditions, everything being divided carefully among the camp.

The camps were each a company of fifty, traveling about a day's journey apart, on account of the feed for the cattle.

Bishop Hunter was very kind to Lydia, and as they neared their journey's end, he would often come up and ride along a moment, saying in his quaint, abrupt fashion:

"Fine boy, fine boy! cattle look well; old cattle! didn't expect 'em to see the valley; look well, look well, better than when they started. Fine boy, fine boy — !"

By this time the worthy man would be out of hearing and soon out of sight, giving his jerky discourse to the winds that blew softly round his little gig.

Lydia's food lasted very well, she sometimes making a little mush or johnny-cake; the cows giving milk night and morning. When there was no fire she would turn the warm milk out on some parched meal, let it soak awhile, and then eat it with thankfulness.

For butter, the "strippins" were taken at night and in the morning, put into the churn which was in the wagon, and at night she would find a little pat of butter sufficient for breakfast, churned by the day's riding.

Days, weeks and months thus passed by, and at last, about the first of October, the train entered Emigration canyon.

Long camping times were now a thing of the past, and all anxiously watched for the first sight of the valley of the Great Salt Lake, where all their hopes were centered, and their feet were bound.

What a joyful cry ascended from the weary travelers as the mouth of the canyon was reached, and they were almost at their journey's end! Oh, what a glorious time was that! Lydia's bosom swelled with unspeakable joy as her eye beheld the scene before her, and she realized that her journey's end was reached.

A general halt was called, and a universal prayer of praise and thanksgiving ascended to that Father who had established the Saints in the tops of the mountains.

After feasting their eyes until somewhat satisfied, every one anxiously hurried to reach this blessed spot, and very soon the long serpentine train was in motion.

Down the declivity cumberously hastened the tired oxen, urged by the loud and oft-repeated "whoa-ha, whoa," of their lusty drivers.

On the third of October, 1850, the company reached the city, then called Great Salt Lake City. Wagons went here and there, friends rushed out from every hut and tent to greet and welcome the travelers.

As Lydia looked around her she was surprised to see the many comfortable homes dotted around, with weighty stacks of grain, and ricks and stacks of wild hay garnered for the winter's use.

Three years only had the Saints been here and already she saw houses and sheds on every hand, with here and there a fence, all the lumber for which had been sawed out by hand.

The long street on which she was traveling was called Emigration street; (now called third South street); it was a distinct line in this wilderness, of houses, cabins and tents; but as there were very few fences, little could be told of the plan of the city as it now stands.

The houses were mostly thatched with straw or covered with mud. Some few shingles had begun to assert their rights by proudly crowning a few of the most pretentious houses.

Lydia enquired the way to her brother-in-law, Joseph W. Johnson's house, to which she directed James to drive. Joseph Johnson had married Newel's sister, and Lydia met a warm welcome from these kind-hearted people.

Here she rested for several days, washing and ironing up her clothes and overlooking the slender stores remaining from the journey.

Samuel, her step-son, was with his uncle, he having left Mr. Wixom because of unkind treatment. He greeted his mother with noisy rejoicings, and immediately began planning for a home, or a start for one, for the family.

"Mother," he said, about the second day of her arrival, "I think we might take a lot somewhere down in the south-eastern part of the city, drive the wagon on it and then make plans for the coming winter."

"Why, my son, do you wish to go down there?"

"Well, mother, you know the cows must have some feed and on the bench close by, there's pretty good feed."

"Well, Samuel, in a couple of days we will hitch up and make a start for a home once more."

Accordingly, on the fourth day of her arrival Lydia directed Samuel and James to yoke up the oxen and cows, and, for the last time for many months, she and her little ones traveled in a wagon.

She called a halt on a vacant lot in what is now the First Ward, took possession of the same and at once made plans for a house. Before making any move to build, however, Lydia went to the agent of the Emigration Fund, delivered up the two yoke of oxen, and gave her note for sixty dollars for the use of them in crossing the plains. Before two years were past this note was redeemed and she was out of debt.

The adobe yard was close by the new home, and one evening as the little circle was gathered round the blazing camp-fire the widow said, "Boys, do you think you could make adobes?"

"Of course we could, mother; Uncle Joseph will show us; you know he is a mason," said Samuel.

"Well, if you boys could make some adobes, and then get a job to pay for laying them up, we might get up one or two rooms which would be warm and comfortable."

Execution followed close upon the heels of plans with the indomitable little woman, and by the beginning of December the house was ready for occupation. Brother Johnson had laid up the walls of the little, two-roomed house for work which the boys did for him. Poles were brought from the canyon to lay across the top of the walls to serve as rafters on which to pile the roof of straw and dirt. From the wagon Lydia had drawn out three window sash, much to the joy of the boys. These had been saved by the mother when leaving the states. These gave two windows to the front and one smaller one to the back room, which latter was used as a bed-room. The doors were made of "shake" (lumber split out of logs instead of sawed), strongly fastened together and hung with rude, home-made hinges; these doors, overhung with a stout blanket, were quite capable of keeping out the cold. A huge fireplace filled up part of one side of the "big room." The floor of earth was oddly carpeted, first with a lavish supply of straw, over which was stretched a rag carpet fastened to numerous stakes driven down all around the edge of the room. For the bed-room the box of the old wagon was split up and the boards were laid down under the beds. When settled, the little family was more comfortable than it had been since leaving Nauvoo.

As soon as possible after moving into the house, Lydia went around to her neighbors and told them she was about to open a small school.

Schools were then very rare, and on the opening day the brave teacher was surprised to see so many pupils present. The school paid so well during the winter, and so satisfied were the people there with the teacher's labors, that she was solicited to accept the Ward school, which she accordingly did in the Spring.

CHAPTER XII

When first moving into their little, home Lydia had put all the cows but one out upon the range. The following very remarkable instance, is an example of what God will do for those who gladly keep His laws:

The one cow left at home stood out in the open air, staked a little way from the house. One morning in December Lydia awoke to find herself surrounded by a mountain of snow.

"Oh the cow!" said Lydia, as she sprang from her bed; "boys, something must be done."

Hurriedly dressing, she went to the door, and there stood the faithful beast, cold and shivering, and there was not a spear of feed to give her.

"Boys, take this blanket," said Lydia taking a heavy, warm, home-made blanket from her bed, "and go down to Bro. Drake, who lives in the Second Ward. I knew him in the Ponca camp, and something whispers to me that he will let us have some feed for the cow. Tell him I would like to get enough of some kind of feed to last until this storm is over, and we can turn the poor thing out. This blanket is a good, almost new one, and should be worth part of a load."

The boys hastened down to Bro. Drake's, and in a little while Lydia was pleased and surprised to see them returning in a wagon, which was well loaded with feed.

You may be sure Lydia thanked and blessed her kind friend; the boys went to work and made a pen of poles which they had hauled for wood, and soon had "bossie" in a warm place.

In the course of a few days, Lydia was able to churn, getting just about a pound of butter. When it was all worked over, she said to the children who had watched the operation with much interest.

"Now children, what shall we do? Here is just about a pound of butter; we may not be able to get the tenth from the cow, and shall we pay this, the first pound for tithing, or will we eat this and trust to luck to get the tenth?"

"Pay this for tithing," answered all the children with one breath. "We can do without, mother, till you churn again."

So the butter was taken to the tithing office; and that Winter Lydia paid tithing on forty pounds of butter, from that cow who was a "stripper;" (had no calf for two years,) and furthermore, the cow never got a spear of feed but what Bro. Drake had brought, it having lasted until the grass grew in the Spring.

As Lydia has since told me, she has made it a firm rule to pay the first instead of the tenth of everything for tithing, commencing always with New Year's day. "And," added she in relating this circumstance, "I have never been without batter in the house from that day to this."

Spring came and went, Summer passed, and Lydia was still teaching.

Let me copy Lydia's own words about the next events of her life.

"Some time in the Fall of '51, a friend by the name of John Dalton proposed to become my protector for this life, if I wished him to do so. He had a farm six miles from the city, which he had no one to live upon, as his first wife lived in the city in a comfortable home. Said I could think of it, and sometime he would call again. This was a new idea to me; for since my dear Newel's death, I had never thought of marrying again. It had been all my study to take care of our little ones, and try to teach them those principles which would prepare them for usefulness in this life, and to meet their father in eternity, so that we might be an unbroken family in the future state of existence.

"What should I do? What would be for our best good?

"My boys had to go from home to get work, and the responsibilities upon me were very heavy. I prayed, I sought to do for the best. I had always believed in the principle of celestial marriage, since I received a testimony of its truth in an early day from the Prophet Joseph's teachings. I have heard him teach it in public as well as in private; have heard him relate the incident of the angel coming to him with a drawn sword, commanding him to obey the law, or he should lose his priesthood as well as his life if he did not go forward in this principle; and I had received a strong testimony of its truth when under the Prophet's teachings. The spirit seemed to whisper to me, you can now test your belief by practice. What would be for the best for my children? If we were situated on a farm, it would give them employment, always at home; and the change would relieve me of many cares and burdens which were fast growing too much for my strength. My constant prayer was, 'Oh Lord give me wisdom to do that which will by Thy will!' At last, I concluded to accept."

Lydia soon found herself, after accepting the proposition, situated on a farm, with plenty of labor for herself and family. She moved in September, '51. In December, '52, a girl was born to her, whom she called Artemesia.

Nearly five years were spent upon this farm, and at the end of that time, Lydia returned to her home in the city; Mr. Dalton having expressed a desire for her to do so. He said she had performed all the labors required of her in an acceptable manner, but she was welcome now to return home.

She had lived under the celestial law, and had found no more trials than she could bear, and she thus gives her testimony concerning the principle:

"It may be some will enquire of me, 'how do you like plurality after living in it and getting the experience you desired? What are your feelings now?' I will say I like it first-rate; my belief is strengthened; I do beleive it is a principle that if not abused, will purify and exalt those that enter into it with purity of purpose, and so abide therein."

On her return to the city, she took up school again, and the people were very glad to have her do so. She began to teach the Ward school in the Spring of '56.

In the early Spring of '58, when rumors of Johnson's army began to come like a blasting air upon these peaceful mountain homes, Pres. Young called out a standing army to prepare for future emergencies. Lydia's oldest daughter, Sally, had married a young man named Zemira Palmer, some two years previous to this, and they were living in Provo. This young man was called to act as a soldier in this standing army, and he wrote to Lydia, asking her if she would not come and live with her daughter, the boys taking charge of the farm. She complied. But very shortly afterwards the standing army was disorganized. Pres. Young had decided to make a complete move from the city, going south, so that when the army should come in, they would find nothing but desolation and lonliness.

The general excitement caused many weak and doubtful spirits to quiver with affright. Among the rest, an old man living in Provo, named Hoops, had become so alarmed that he was determined to leave Utah at any cost.

One morning Zemira came in and said, "Well Sally, old man Hoops is going to sell out if he can, *give out* if he can't *sell* out, and *get* out whether or not. He has a good farm, a city lot and tolerably good house, but nothing will keep him here."

As he ceased speaking, the spirit whispered to Lydia, "The hand of the Lord is in this. Because of your faithfulness in the past, you shall have a good home. Go, and you shall obtain this for yourself and children."

Presently she said quietly to James who was with her:

"Are you acquainted with this old gentleman, Hoops?"

"Yes, mother; why?"

"Zemira will not need us here now, and as we do not wish to return to the city in the present state of things, I thought perhaps we might be able to buy this place of the old man."

"Why, mother, all we have would not begin to buy the place. It's worth several hundred dollars. It would be an imposition to ask the old man to take a wagon and what few other things we could give him. I could not bring my feelings to consent to such an imposition."

Lydia felt that she knew that when she listened to the guidings of that Spirit which had so often prompted her, that she had always succeeded and been prospered; and she was sure, although it looked hopeless, that she would succeed now.

Waiting a little while, she next asked Zemira if he would go with her and introduce her to Bro. Hoops.

With a peculiar smile he answered,

"Yes, mother, I will go with you, if you really wish it, but I have no faith that you can possibly get the place."

They went down to the old man's place and Lydia stated to him the object of her visit. He asked her what she had, and as she named over the various articles she could turn out, he said:

"That's just what I want."

And when she had told him all she had to give, he eagerly answered, "It's a bargain."

So she was once more in possession of a good home.

Just before leaving the city for Provo, Lydia had gone to President Young and stated her circumstances in full to him, and asked if he knew any reason why she should not have a divorce from Mr. Dalton. She had then been separated from him for some time The President did not know anything to prevent her being a free woman, and accordingly gave her a legal divorce. So she was once more alone and battling with life without earthly aid.

Her farm was a good one, and with the valuable assistance of her boys, she soon became comfortable.

A widower, named McClellan, was living at this time in Payson who had two motherless girls, aged eleven and thirteen. He was comfortably situated, and, becoming acquainted with Lydia, he very much admired her kind, motherly ways and general thriftiness, and he besought her to unite her fortunes with his and be a mother to his girls who had been orphaned about two years previously.

Lydia was not very willing to once more embark upon the perilous sea of matrimony. Her heart was buried with her husband, and no love ever had or ever could waken it to life. She had had a sorrowful experience in that state with Mr. Dalton, and as she was now getting in years, being upwards of fifty, she shrank from again taking a wife's burdens upon her. Still, her heart yearned over the little helpless, motherless girls. Finally, after much serious thought, she again accepted an earthly companion, and joined her fate, for time, with James McClellan.

They moved to Payson in '60, where his farm was situated. Two or three years after this Bro. McClellan was called south, and Lydia moved with him, leaving Jesse and Hyrum with their brother James in Provo. They settled at the Santa Clara, and soon became very nicely fixed.

In the Fall of 71, Lydia's brother, Jesse, wrote to her that their father and mother were both dead, and, as there was some property to be divided among the children, she had better visit the old homestead where he lived and get her share.

She therefore went east and was treated very kindly by her brothers and sisters and enjoyed herself quite well. As her share she received $1,500, and then returned home.

On the 1st of January, 1877, work was commenced in the St. George temple. President Young called upon Lydia to act as one of the workers. Circumstances beyond her control did not permit her to go until the Fall of '77, when she entered the sacred walls as one of the regular attendants.

In the Winter of '79-80 Brother McClellan's health failed altogether, and on the 10th of February, 1880, he died. Thus, after a companionship of twenty years, Lydia was once more a widow. The work in the temple, however, was so constant and pleasant that she could not feel lonely.

In 1882 Lydia purchased a piece of property in St. George and has there settled. She shut up her house in Santa Clara, and manages to live quite comfortably with the proceeds of her little estate.

She is all alone, as Samuel lives in Santa Clara; Sally and Lydia, with their husbands, in Orderville; Newel, in Provo; James, Jesse and Artemesia, in Payson; Joseph went to Arizona and died there four years ago, and Hyrum died at Payson three years ago unmarried.

Her posterity are numerous; they outnumber that of her eleven brothers and sisters put together. She has upwards of eighty children, grand-children and great grand-children, and is proud of her labors and the "helps" she has raised to assist in the upbuilding of this kingdom.

When the relief society was organized by the Prophet Joseph in Nauvoo, Lydia was one of its active members, and from that time until now she has almost continuously labored in one of these societies.

In the old-time fairs she has often taken prizes for the production of her hands. She has always taken a very active interest in sericulture since its introduction into this territory. There is now on exhibition in the Philadelphia silk rooms several silk skeins of various colors so well spun and twisted as to be indistinguishable from the imported article; also nets, mits, etc., of Lydia's make.

Her labors in the temple are constant and full of the greatest joy and pleasure. She has labored there as a work-hand 621 days, has received endowments for over 700 of her dead and those of her friends; and has blessed many sick, sorrowful and afflicted. Shall I paint a little scene of almost daily occurrence during the past season in St. George?

Tall trees shade a modest house so deeply set in its leafy frame that the passer-by scarcely discerns its shape. Birds sing in their bright green home, and the grass hides many a harmless insect. The dewy freshness of the morning shimmers on every bough and grassy hillock. The chickens cluck over their morning meal; the cow stands in her cosy shed, happy with her dewy green breakfast and chewing the cud in contentment.

Out of the front door steps a brisk little woman with so blithe an air, and free a step that you are surprised to look under the veiled bonnet and find a kind, withered face surrounded with a silvery halo of pure white hair. The firm lines around the mouth are rather deepened with experience, but the lips wear that pleasant half-smile seen on the faces of the cheerful; the blue eyes, a little dimmed with age and tears, but full of a sunny light; and the expression so soft and sweet that little children love to kiss the dear old face. Over the path goes she, and steps into the waiting temple carriage before the clock strikes eight; her house as neat as wax, everything about her clean, happy and well fed. This is Lydia, now seventy-one years old, and living alone, but for the beloved spirits of Newel and her children who often visit her in dreams and visions. She has earned her present peace and rest, and to-day, as it passes, is but the one link less between her and her longed-for, eternal home with her beloved husband. But it is a very golden link, for it is gilded with precious blessings and privileges but few mortals enjoy. She blesses and is blessed.

And here let us leave her, with the prayer to know and greet her when we shall be united on the glorious resurrection day!